I HEAR

HIS

CALL

*Devotional Thoughts for Women
on Following God*

ANITA CORRINE
DONIHUE

BARBOUR BOOKS
An Imprint of Barbour Publishing, Inc.

WHEN
I HEAR
HIS
CALL

Published by Barbour Books, an imprint of Barbour Publishing, Inc., P.O. Box 719, Uhrichsville, Ohio 44683, www.barbourbooks.com

Member of the
Evangelical Christian
Publishers Association

Printed in the United States of America.

DEDICATION

Special thanks and deepest gratitude
go to my friend, Lorian Choate—
for help in polishing *When I Hear His Call,*
for her sensitivity toward the needs of others,
and for the quiet, caring way she responds.

CONTENTS

Contents

INTRODUCTION

Being confident of this,
that he who began a good work
in you will carry it on to completion
until the day of Christ Jesus. . . .
For it is God who works in you to will and
to act according to his good purpose. . . .
I can do everything through him
who gives me strength.
PHILIPPIANS 1:6; 2:13; 4:13 NIV

I am sitting in my living room chair, thinking of those for whom *When I Hear His Call* was written. The winter sun is peering over the top of Mount Rainier and pushing its way through a multitude of clouds. Its rays are casting a rosy, gentle radiance across the sky, framing each cloud with a pink, lacy border. We have been told a red sky in the morning predicts rainstorms, yet God is still in charge.

When God calls, His voice rings out true and clear as He makes a way over our mountains and through our clouds to the point where we can hear Him calling us on to our next journey with Him. Yet like the sunrise, He helps prepare us for the gentle rose-strewn or stormy days. The best part is the way our Lord Jesus walks ahead of us. All we need do is cling to the hem of His garment.

Some of God's calls appear special, like going to a foreign land as a missionary or being called to the ministry. However, God gives us equally important calls on a daily basis. Some may seem insignificant, yet all have the potential to impact lives around us.

We may wonder why we don't always hear God's invitation. But the Bible says, "For many are called, but few are chosen" (Matthew 22:14 NKJV).

We must continually tune in to God, search for His reassuring presence, and learn to recognize His voice. He has a way of reaching over our obstacles and distractions. He is able to break through disappointment and insecurity and meet with us one on one—but only if we allow Him to do so.

When we answer God's call, He is free to help us remove every hindrance from the course He directs us to take.

My prayer for you is that God will richly bless you as you hear and recognize His call to a wonderful adventure with Him.

LET ME HEAR YOUR CALL

Father, I love You with all my heart. Although I am fearful of what may lie ahead, I long for You to lead me.

What have I to offer? Do You really have a plan for me in this uncertain, crazy world? Because I am Your child, I know You have already begun a good work in me. Let me hear Your call, so it can be carried on to fulfillment.

Please don't allow me to run ahead of You and conjure my own ideas, lest I be unable to follow Your path. Help me not to drag my feet when You bid and miss an opportunity to serve, as I yield to Your will and act in accordance with Your purpose.

Give me a dream, I pray. Help me acknowledge it. Move my dream forward until it becomes a vision. Show me what You want me to do. I am eager to follow You on this journey, and I anticipate great things. I will trust You to remove barriers and surround me with Your protective presence, as we begin our glorious walk together.

Thank You, Lord, for leading me every step of the way. In Jesus' name, amen.

*New
Life*

ACCEPTING CHRIST

And when the Pharisees saw it, they said to His disciples, "Why does your Teacher eat with tax collectors and sinners?"

When Jesus heard that, He said to them, "Those who are well have no need of a physician, but those who are sick. But go and learn what this means: 'I desire mercy and not sacrifice.' For I did not come to call the righteous, but sinners, to repentance."

MATTHEW 9:11–13 NKJV

TRANSFORMED LIFE

She was brought into this world with help from a Polish midwife. The daughter of an African-American mother who had been raped, the baby girl soon came to favor her mother's tall, large-boned build. As she grew, though, shuffling from one place to another left her without a sense of attachment. She felt neither loved nor wanted.

When her mother could care for her no longer, the child was sent to live with Dr. and Mrs. Bell and their ten children.

Dr. Bell was the preacher at a small church in downtown Philadelphia, where the young girl learned many old-time hymns. Yet, in spite of Dr. and Mrs. Bell's attempts to be a good influence, the allure of Philadelphia's mean streets was too powerful. To survive out there, she knew she had to be tough. She beat up anyone who crossed her, and soon she had acquired a bad reputation. By the time she turned twelve, she had become a street gang ringleader.

Still, her love for music kept her attending church. The Christian influence and faithful prayers from those who cared about her slowly began to pay off. One Sunday morning in a little Chester, Pennsylvania, church, the struggling adolescent girl gave her heart to the Lord. Her life changed immediately. The church folks treated her like family. Between her Christian friends and the beloved Dr. and Mrs. Bell, she finally realized what it meant to be loved.

When she became a young adult, she had an argument with another member of the congregation and strayed from the church. During those years her singing talent developed, eventually bringing her fame as a vocal entertainer in nightclubs and on television. Yet, despite her newfound fame, sadness and a longing for a closer walk with God dogged her continually.

One night, she turned on her radio and a man by the name of Billy Graham was talking. His message, which began with "The Bible says," touched her hungry heart.

While fulfilling singing engagements in New York, she discovered the Billy Graham Crusade was coming to Madison Square Garden. She wanted to attend but didn't know how she could fit it into her schedule.

A few days later when she appeared on a TV show, the subject of the Billy Graham Crusade again came up. She felt a tremendous drive to go to that crusade. Without hesitation, she said right on the air that she wanted to hear Billy Graham speak.

After she returned to her hotel room, the phone rang. It was a member from the Billy Graham Crusade team, offering her ten tickets. The tickets would make it possible for her not to have to wait in a long line. It was then she realized she had told millions that she wanted to attend the crusade.

Madison Square Garden wasn't new to her. She had performed several benefit shows there before thousands of people. This time when she entered, though, the arena was different. She was filled with wonder.

The choir opened the crusade by singing "This Is My Story." At that moment, the young woman remembered singing that very same song with the little church congregation in Chester. Love and friendship filled the air as she listened.

The woman clung to Billy Graham's message from God's Word. She felt like a hungry baby bird receiving one morsel of spiritual food at a time. God had begun calling her to drink from His cup of living water. She knew she needed to get things right with Him.

She returned to the crusade each night she had an opportunity. Every evening, Billy Graham's message hit her like lightning, and she drew a little closer to God. Every day, she counted the hours until she could return and hear sermons of life and forgiveness.

She was surprised when she was invited to sing with the crusade choir. Even though she told Billy Graham's team she didn't have things right with God, they encouraged her to sing. Surrounded by choir leader Cliff Barrows, singer George Beverly Shea, and caring Christians, her soul was fed and blessed.

The tremendous turnout resulted in the crusade meetings being extended eight more weeks. She knew she must return to touring, but she decided to go one last night and hear one more message from God's Word.

While sitting at the crusade, she recognized God was showing her a better place to sing. Instead of appearing in nightclubs, He was calling her to use her talents for Him. She just didn't know how it could be possible. Money was scarce. Times were tough. She sat there silently arguing with the Lord. How could singing for God ever become a reality?

Before she knew what was happening, Cliff Barrows's familiar voice rang out over the speakers, inviting her to sing "His Eye Is on the Sparrow" for the crusade audience. What could she say? The only answer was yes.

She was so nervous she thought her heart would stop beating. Although she had performed

"His Eye Is on the Sparrow" many times, this was unlike anything she had ever experienced.

In spite of her uneasiness, she stepped up to the microphone with dignity and grace. No matter how scared she felt, her professional experience took over. Still, something was happening inside her. She realized the two different lives she was leading could not coexist. She must make a choice. She couldn't be on both sides of the fence in God's eyes.

Ethel Waters finished singing, sat down and paused for a moment, and then rededicated her heart to Jesus. A marvelous, forgiving presence filled her, followed by a peace she had never known. The bad was gone, replaced by God's goodness. The hurt and bitterness she had stored up through her life melted away.

Ethel continued singing at the meetings instead of returning to work. Even though she didn't know how she could make a living by using her voice for the Lord, she fought her doubts and kept committing everything to God. Ethel did know one thing. He *would* provide. She returned home and cancelled her club engagements.

Many people heard Ethel Waters sing on national television with the Billy Graham Crusade and God opened doors. She sang for Youth for Christ crusades throughout the country, the Tennessee Ernie Ford TV show, and the Dale Evans and Roy Rogers TV series. Each time Ethel sang "His Eye Is on the Sparrow," she told how much she loved God and what He had done for her.

She was also called to sing "Deep River," "Just a Closer Walk with Thee," "Nobody Knows the Trouble I've Seen," and many other spiritual favorites.

Because Ethel Waters heeded God's call to accept Him as her Savior, He used her Christian witness in example and song. Her God-inspired influence spanned several generations, enabling her to reach millions of lives, young and old. Always, she passed on God's love in her own inimitable way.

BEGINNING THE ADVENTURE

The next day John [the Baptist] was there again with two of his disciples. When he saw Jesus passing by, he said, "Look, the Lamb of God!"

When the two disciples heard him say this, they followed Jesus.

JOHN 1:35–37 NIV

LIFE CHANGES

Andrew, a strong, rough-hewn fisherman, was living proof of his name's Greek meaning—manliness. It took brawn and grit to drag heavy fish-filled nets and battle enormous waves on the Sea of Galilee.

But there was another side to the manly Andrew.

He was a loving and devoted brother and a disciple of John the Baptist.

Andrew's day of days probably began like any other. Then something happened as Andrew and another disciple stood with their friend John the Baptist, something that changed Andrew's life. A holy presence walked by. Jesus. No other compared with this Man.

John the Baptist pointed toward Jesus and said, "Behold the Lamb of God!" Was that a gentle hint to go seek the Savior?

The Lamb of God? What could this mean? Lambs were used for sacrifice. Did John's enlightening words open Andrew's eyes? Who was this Man that He could be called such? Was God calling Andrew to leave John and follow Jesus?

When the two disciples caught up with the Master, Jesus turned around and asked what they wanted. Andrew didn't hesitate. He desired to talk with Jesus privately and asked where the Master lived.

Jesus invited both of the disciples to His home. No one knows what Jesus and the two men discussed.

When Andrew left Jesus' home, he believed that the *Lamb of God* was truly the *Son of God* and immediately became one of the Savior's first followers.

Did the burly fisherman feel awestruck when he hurried away to find his brother, Peter? He rushed to tell Peter the news and bring him back to meet the Messiah. Andrew was obviously over-joyed to present his brother to the Lord.

Perhaps Andrew and Peter knew of Jesus through the teachings of John the Baptist. Now they were able to talk and learn from the Master personally!

The brothers continued their fishing business for awhile. We only know that they were working with their nets when they looked up to find Jesus standing before them.

The Lord's firm words, "Come, follow me, . . . and I will make you fishers of men" (Mark 1:17 NIV) probably sent chills down Andrew's spine. Without debate, he dropped his nets and led the way for Peter, James, and John to follow the Lord.

Andrew was among the twelve men Jesus appointed to become apostles. Imagine the wonder he felt when he was instructed to go out and preach, heal the sick, and cast out demons in Jesus' name!

Andrew didn't do things heedlessly. He spent time asking questions of Jesus and listening to the Lord talk about God's plans for the future.

Andrew's actions didn't bring him much attention or praise. Instead, this quiet, faithful apostle became known for introducing people to Jesus and looking for ways to help. He brought the boy with the loaves and fishes to Jesus so that five thousand men, plus women and children, could be fed. He and Philip brought several Greeks to Jesus so they could worship the Lord.

Like the disciples, we too can hear Jesus calling,

"Come, follow Me." What we do may not be as profound as the work Peter was given. We may simply be called, as Andrew was, to bring folks to the Lord, one person at a time, quietly and lovingly.

No matter how the Lord uses us, we can be a part of a life-changing adventure when we walk with Him.

GROWING IN CHRIST

Therefore, if anyone is in Christ, he is a new creation; the old has gone, the new has come! 2 CORINTHIANS 5:17 NIV

FINDING THE RIGHT COURSE

The morning sun shone crystal clear through the window of my friend Mary's lovely hilltop home and crept silently across the Auburn valley. I had spent the night at Mary's house and awakened before anyone else. I restlessly gazed out the window, pondering what my future would hold.

Eighteen years old, I had graduated from high school and landed a job as a stenographer at the Renton Boeing plant. I should have felt a sense of satisfaction, but something was missing.

I stood there reminiscing about my growing-up years. I had accepted Jesus as my Savior at the early age of seven in an after-school Child

Evangelism Good News Club. *That was a great beginning with the Lord,* I thought. It didn't take long, however, for my conscience to remind me of all the spiritual ups and downs I had experienced, especially during my teenage years.

I thought about my Christian grandma. She often let me spend summer vacations with her, and we became close. When my teenage years approached, Grandma and I had quite a tug-of-war over Christian standards.

"Anita, you might be a Christian, but you aren't a dedicated Christian," Grandma said, never one to mince words. "That just isn't good enough. Pray it through. Give your all to God."

At the time, her perceptive words made me angry and frustrated. I spluttered back at Grandma, but at the same time I knew deep inside that she was seriously holding me up in prayer. I love and appreciate her to this day for that.

I was always good at blaming others for my shortcomings. Now as I stood at the window, I realized I was standing on the threshold of adulthood. No longer could I blame anyone else for my faults. I must make the right choices and build a solid adult life.

When I heard Mary's mother in the kitchen, I paid no attention, still deep in my thoughts. Softly, Mary's mom came up to the window and stood beside me. She put her hand on my shoulder and stood by silently for a few minutes.

I could tell she was weighing her words before

she finally spoke. "Look down there, Anita." She pointed toward the valley. "That's the Green River winding its way through the countryside. Your life is going to be like that. You are beginning a brand-new adventure. Let God help you make the right choices. If you stay on course with Him, all will be well."

A few months later, I knelt beside my bed and rededicated my messed-up, yo-yo life to God. Immediately, I felt a huge weight lift from my shoulders. New joy filled me through and through, joy I had never experienced before. Later I learned that enthusiastic new presence in me was God's wonderful, cleansing, freeing Holy Spirit. Before then, I was afraid or ashamed to tell people I was a Christian. Things were different after that glorious night. I was so excited about what God did for me, I had to tell everyone who would listen.

The new adventure did begin. It was as though God had rolled out a map, His holy Word, and charted a course on my river of life. He provided safe and sure passages for me to travel.

After all these years, I still continue to sense His hand on my shoulder as He guides me along the way through each new quest with Him. Sometimes this river of life is smooth as glass, but frequently I face rough waters. God has to remind me not to be careless when life goes my way, and to heed His direction and not panic when life gets rough.

God has a new adventure awaiting me every day. He opens doors I never dreamed possible. He heals my hurts. He cares for my concerns. He frees me from fear. He transforms my temptations to triumph. Best of all, He gives me abundant life in all circumstances with a deep, endless joy from His Holy Spirit. For this, I never cease to thank Him.

Perhaps you are at a turning point in your life, trying to decide which way to go. God has a wonderful adventure in store for you—if you are willing to give your all and place your life in His capable hands.

The same God who is able to move mountains, rivers, and even ocean waves is tenderly reaching out and inviting you to follow Him. Choose His course. Learn from Him. Obey Him. Draw close to Him and grow spiritually. Then experience His tender love and His tremendous power working in your life.

I HEARD THE VOICE OF JESUS SAY

I heard the voice of Jesus say,
"Behold, I freely give
The living water; thirsty one,
Stoop down and drink, and live."
I came to Jesus, and I drank
Of that life-giving stream;
My thirst was quenched, my soul revived,
And now I live in Him.

HORATIUS BONAR, 1808–1889

CREATE IN ME A STAINLESS HEART

O Lord, my God, have mercy upon me, I pray. Though I try to do what is right, I often fall short. I can't build a victorious life without You. Forgive me of my short-comings and wrong attitudes. I long to be acceptable in Your sight.

Sprinkle Your cleansing blood upon my heart. Wash and make me as white as snow. Refine me. Skim off my faults and make Your child pure like glistening gold. Create in me a stainless heart, O Lord. Restore a just spirit within my soul. Thank You for not losing patience or giving up on one such as I. Fill me with Your Holy Spirit, and restore to my life the joy of Your salvation.

As You and I begin this new quest in life, I pray for You to help me be careful and obedient in all I think, say, and do. I want to exalt You with my whole being, Lord.

I will sing with joy about Your love and forgiveness. My lips will constantly praise You through every adventure of my life. I want to pass on Your good news to all who are willing to listen.

Thank You, Lord, for being my Savior!

Seek
Him

Stop

But those who wait on the LORD
Shall renew their strength;
They shall mount up with wings like
    eagles,
They shall run and not be weary,
They shall walk and not faint.

                     ISAIAH 40:31 NKJV

GETTING AHEAD OF GOD

I have a terrible sense of direction. My family tells me I can get lost turning around twice with no trouble at all. Whenever Bob and I go for drives, he coaches me on how to find the right way and locate north while turning different directions. (I can find north as long as the sun is out.)

Once I was scheduled to attend a meeting about forty-five minutes from our town. Bob drew a map for me ahead of time with north in the appropriate spot. For some reason, the map made more sense when I looked at it upside down! After all, I was facing south when I read it.

It was important for me to be on time, so I left early in case I got lost. Since I had already studied the directions ahead of time, I stuffed them in my purse and was off. The trip would be a piece of cake! Now I could enjoy my favorite Christian radio station for a whole hour with no interruptions.

The freeway gave me no problem. I knew which exit to take and I reached it ahead of time. *I'm not so bad at this,* I thought. I remembered I was to go three miles through town and turn on a street named Jasper.

I drove three miles. No Jasper in sight. Two miles more. Still no luck. Before I knew it, I began frantically turning right and left and had no idea where I was or which way was north. (After all, how could I find north when it was cloudy?) I was so frustrated by this time that I was almost in tears. I was lost. Again.

It suddenly dawned on me that I needed to pull over, stop, and read the map. I sat on the side of a country road in the middle of nowhere and studied the map Bob had carefully made for me.

Then I bowed my head and asked God to help me find my way.

At that moment, the sun crept from behind the clouds. Seeing it made me feel a little better. I took a deep breath and somehow worked my way back to town, carefully following the directions. *It's a good thing I left early,* I thought.

Before long I arrived at the correct house and pulled in the driveway. I was right on time. I checked my hair and makeup in the car mirror and casually walked to the door.

The hostess greeted me with a smile. "Hi, Anita. I'm glad you're here. Did you have any trouble finding my home?"

I smiled back, removing my coat. "I got turned

around a little, but Bob's map kept me on the right track."

That day I made a promise to stop and pay closer attention to directions before leaving for new destinations.

Many of us hear God's call and are thrilled at what He wants us to do. We get so excited we want to jump in and change the world without awaiting directions. Before long we look around and wonder why everything is going wrong and where God is in this process.

God doesn't just call us. He often carefully prepares us for what He wants us to do. It's extremely important for us to stop and await further instructions from Him. We may need to tarry a few hours, days, months, or even years. Remember that Jesus waited thirty years for God's plan to be fulfilled.

It is as important to wait and allow God to groom us for His work as it is to heed His call in the first place.

As we learn to patiently listen, pray, and take plenty of time to study the Bible, we will be able to serve Him in a far better way than if we were to rush out on our own.

There may be times after we begin serving Him when we think we have it all figured out. Too often, though, we make a wrong turn. That is the time to stop and once again pull out God's Word, pray for a calm head, and review His directions.

We need to linger with Him for as long as needed. We must be patient. As we wait on God, He restores our strength. We will ascend on His wings as baby eagles. Our surety and strength will increase. Our racing minds and hearts will quiet.

He is the One who shows us the way.

LOOK

How sweet are Your words to my taste,
Sweeter than honey to my mouth!
Through Your precepts I get understanding;
Therefore I hate every false way.

Your word is a lamp to my feet
And a light to my path.
I have sworn and confirmed
That I will keep Your righteous judgments.

I am afflicted very much;
Revive me, O LORD, according to Your word.

Accept, I pray, the freewill offerings
Of my mouth, O LORD,
And teach me Your judgments.

PSALM 119:103–108 NKJV

Do you ever long with all your heart to serve God but aren't sure which way He is leading you?

E. E. Byrum once told a story of a miner who tramped through the mountains in search of precious metal. When the miner came to a small waterfall, he was so entranced by the clear, sparkling falls that cascaded from the rocky crevasse to a gurgling stream that he drew closer and dipped in his cup for a cool drink.

When he bent down, he was astonished to discover glistening rocks sprinkled throughout the pebbled floor. He followed the stream, hoping he would be able to find its hidden riches.

New energy surged through the miner as he fervently labored along the bank. He could already visualize himself becoming wealthy.

Farther along, the stream split into numerous little brooks. Which way should he go? He wondered if his search would come to a fruitless end. Still, he did not give up.

The prospector went to town, bought a crucible, and returned to where he had left off. With rigorous care, he ran loads of rock through a fiery melting process. Carefully and patiently, he removed the dross. Finally, after many days of hard labor, pure gold emerged. The determined miner became wealthier than he ever imagined, all because he wouldn't give up his search.

Byrum went on to explain how in a sense that's

the way it is in our lives as Christians. When we drink from the stream of cleansing, living water of God's Word, we become spiritually wealthier and happier than we could ever have imagined.

There may be times our quest to serve Him is jumbled with obstacles that hide the clarity of His leading. Poverty, illness, and overwhelming discouragement might squeeze into our valley's life-giving stream.

When this happens, we call upon God again and again to lead and strengthen. We often are required to wait patiently (or impatiently) on Him for direction. We plead. We cry. We pray some more, and we wait some more. In spite of not knowing which way to go, we are determined to be faithful and obedient to Him and not move ahead without His leading.

Then the blessings miraculously roll in like timely ocean waves. Our weary souls yield to His purpose of simply being His children. We do not know His ways, but God uses those challenging obstacles to make us strong. He utilizes the heat of our trials to melt away our pride and preconceived ideas. He carefully and lovingly skims off our faults and failures and casts them away farther than the East is from the West.

Through all, God brings forth the priceless worth in us. And, oh, the glory His Holy Spirit rains upon our lives! Oh, the power He places within us! *His* wisdom. *His* power. *His* love.

When this happens, we are in His holy

Presence. It is there He shows us where and how to move forward and best serve and glorify Him.

LISTEN

"Do not leave Jerusalem, but wait for the gift my Father promised, which you have heard me speak about. For John baptized with water, but in a few days you will be baptized with the Holy Spirit."....

When the day of Pentecost came, they were all together in one place. Suddenly a sound like the blowing of a violent wind came from heaven and filled the whole house where they were sitting. They saw what seemed to be tongues of fire that separated and came to rest on each of them. All of them were filled with the Holy Spirit and began to speak in other tongues as the Spirit enabled them.

ACTS 1:4–5; 2:1–4 NIV

MIGHTY WINDS BLOWING

The disciples bade their beloved Master farewell and watched Him ascend to heaven. Afterward, they obeyed His instructions to wait in Jerusalem and pray for the presence of God's Holy Spirit. Before, they had given God a portion of their crops.

Now the followers of Jesus were offering God their entire lives.

Many people were gathered in Jerusalem at this time. Disciples of Jesus, faithful women, Jesus' mother, Mary, and His brothers, and other Christians were all earnestly praying. There was a great sense of expectation as they waited for God's Holy Spirit, the Comforter, to come.

In order for this to happen, their hearts had to be clean. Old things not pleasing to God were released. All in their lives became new.

Sincere prayer intensified. The people pled for holy power and unconditional love to come from on high, the elements only God could supply. How desperately they needed His presence during those troubled times!

Christians prayed with united hearts when the powerful winds came. Could they hear them approaching? Or did the mighty blast suddenly sweep violently through their midst? Could the winds have been so strong that the doors and furniture shook? The Spirit's mighty rush must have stirred the soul of every praying believer.

The Holy Spirit settled upon those present like sanctifying tongues of fire, just as John the Baptist had prophesied. For the first time, those assembled were actually meeting the Comforter—God's presence. He would never leave them.

The glory of the Lord descended upon them and filled them to overflowing. This experience surely empowered the lives of all followers there.

Christians began fearlessly praising God with no concern about what anyone else would think.

The Jerusalem population represented a variety of cultures and spoken languages. People from throughout the Roman world were either visiting or abiding in Jerusalem during this time. Some individuals were devout and prominent.

Amazingly, languages understood by all came from the lips of those people, telling of God's astounding works. The rushing winds, tongues of fire, and excited shouts of praise created great commotion, so much so that multitudes were drawn to the assembly. Everyone present, regardless of ethnic background, heard what was said in his or her own language.

Yes, everyone heard—but how many listened? Only those with open hearts acknowledged the priceless words God spoke to their souls.

Some mocked the worshipers, accusing them of being drunk. Peter, though, boldly stood with the other disciples by his side. He reminded the taunters it was only the third hour—about nine in the morning. Peter recalled God's promise to pour out His Spirit on all people—men *and* women, even servants. Their sons and daughters would prophesy, their old men dream dreams, their young men see visions. God would show wonders in the heavens and on earth. Everyone who called on the Lord would be saved.

Peter admonished the troublemakers that Jesus, whom they had seen performing miracles, had been sent by God, captured illegally, and put to death. He explained that even death couldn't stop Jesus. The Son of God overcame it all and was eternally alive in heaven!

God's love shone in Peter as he not only revealed the terrors of sin but the joy of God's saving grace. His words vigorously rang out on the day of Pentecost and continue to speak to us today. No matter the fears for today or anxieties about tomorrow, whether we be high above the sky or beneath the deepest ocean, nothing can separate us from God's love. Nothing, because Jesus Christ died to make it so, for every single soul.

"BREATHE ON ME, BREATH OF GOD"

Breathe on me, breath of God,
Fill me with life anew,
That I may love what Thou dost love
And do what Thou wouldst do.

EDWIN HATCH (1835–1889)

LET ME HEAR YOUR WINDS

Father, here I am in gridlock freeway traffic, hemmed in on all sides. I've been going full-speed ahead the past few days and have barely taken time to spend with You. My only excuse? There has been so much to do.

Now I'm at a standstill. I don't know what the problem is ahead, but these cars aren't moving an inch. I switch off my engine. In the sanctuary of my car, all grows silent. The world around me stops. It reminds me of those scenes in movies when everything is frozen in motion.

Anxiety and stress leave me as I center my thoughts on You, my almighty God. I pull out my Bible from the glove box and read Your illuminating Word. Your Scriptures saturate my thirsty soul. My heart opens wide to Your holy presence.

Forgive me, Lord, for putting off this precious time with You. Take hold of my deeply rooted faults. Prune them and grant me freedom from wrong motives and actions.

Let me hear the winds of Your Holy Spirit speak to me. Teach me Your lessons. Reveal to me the secrets I must know in order to triumph over life's challenges and be a victorious Christian. Allow me to dream Your dreams and see Your visions.

I praise You for causing Your winds to swirl within me and fill every crack and cranny of my being. You, Lord, are so great and mighty. I can barely contain Your comfort and love as You fill my

heart to the brim and overflowing. Thank
You for the way Your glory, power, and
righteousness surround me.

The world suddenly comes off freeze
mode into real time. Traffic edges for-
ward. Thank You, Lord, for stopping me
in my tracks so I can take in the lessons
of Your Word. I praise You for helping me
draw close and listen to Your leading.
Thank You for enabling me to hear the
winds of Your Holy Spirit stir within my
soul.

Trust
and Obey

PAST

*But one thing I do, forgetting those
things which are behind and reaching
forward to those things which are ahead,
I press toward the goal for the prize of
the upward call of God in Christ Jesus.*

PHILIPPIANS 3:13–14 NKJV

KATHLEEN

Eighteen-year-old Kathleen juggled a cup of coffee in one hand and with her other, pushed open the window curtain of her luxurious Seattle third-floor studio apartment.

Icy flurries swirled in and out through the bare trees in the courtyard below. Sharp gusts of wind pushed white powdery blankets across the sidewalks and streets, carelessly tossing them into the winds bound for nearby Lake Union.

Kathleen shuddered as she recalled a year before when she was homeless. At times, if she couldn't make it to the shelter before it closed, there was no choice but to sleep on the downtown streets. And then she thought of Bruce. When she met him, Kathleen thought he would be her friend, but he had just used her to make money.

Kathleen crumpled into her overstuffed chair near the window and set her empty cup on the table. She covered her face with her hands and began to sob as bitter memories flooded over her. Kathleen had allowed her body to be violated more times than she could remember. She knew it was her own doing: Prostitution brought in plenty of money and provided her with a luxurious place to live.

As Kathleen picked up the new Bible she had tucked in her purse, tears dripped from her eyelashes onto its cover. She turned to verses she had recently discovered—John 3:16–17 (KJV):

> For God so loved the world, that he gave
> his only begotten Son, that whosoever
> believeth in him should not perish, but
> have everlasting life. For God sent not
> his Son into the world to condemn the
> world; but that the world through him
> might be saved.

Kathleen leaned her head back against the chair and thought of how much God must love her. He was making a way for her to have not only everlasting life, but a *new life* with Him as her guide. She was thankful for Susan, her new friend from the mission, and for how Susan had helped her only two days before to ask Jesus into her heart. It was Susan who had given her the new Bible. How grateful she was that God forgave her sins! Now could she ever learn to forgive herself?

She peered out the curtain again. Somewhere above the lake, snow flurries, and clouded morning sky was the sun. Better yet was the assurance of how the *Son of God* was helping her out of her dismal life.

Kathleen glanced at her watch and the boxes stacked around her. Susan would be arriving soon. Kathleen knew if they hurried, she and Susan could have her belongings loaded in Susan's van and be out of town before Bruce called. Since she had the last two nights off, Kathleen was certain he would have a list of customers and instructions ready for her. She shuddered, thinking of his abusive ways, especially when he became angry.

"God, help me. Don't let him find me," she frantically whispered.

She scribbled a note. It was good-bye forever.

Six months seemed like a lifetime since Kathleen's move from Seattle to a small town. She loved Susan's parents and their modest home, where she now paid room and board. Moreover, Susan's church accepted and loved Kathleen. They even helped her find a job at a local clothing store. She was gradually getting on her feet and would soon be able to move into her own place.

In spite of all the good in her life, Kathleen felt terribly lonely. Many of her new friends were married or engaged. She felt out of place, like a fifth wheel. Again, Kathleen took her need to the Lord in prayer.

God answered through a phone call from her pastor, who asked her to serve on a committee to start a Christian singles group in their church. The group would begin with home Bible studies and a church school class.

Three months later, Kathleen grabbed the phone in her new apartment as she was about to dash out the door. She made arrangements to call back a new member of the singles group.

Hanging up, Kathleen glanced in the mirror. Her long black hair fell smoothly over her slim shoulders. The light blue suit she wore accented the blue in her eyes. She glowed with the joy of the Lord. Step by step, He had helped her not only to accept His forgiveness, but to forgive herself of her past. She was finally able to put everything behind her—forever. Now Kathleen realized she really wasn't a fifth wheel. Instead, she was part of the body of Christ.

She couldn't believe how He was using her to bless others. In only an hour, she was scheduled to give her testimony to a large church group in a neighboring town. She knew she would not be giving it alone. God would be with her.

Over the next several years, Kathleen played a major part in organizing several Christian singles groups throughout the surrounding areas. She never stopped thanking God for Susan, who introduced her to the Lord and showed her what it meant to be loved by God and His family.

PRESENT

You see then that a man is justified by works, and not by faith only. Likewise, was not Rahab the harlot also justified by works when she received the messengers and sent them out another way? For as the body without the spirit is dead, so faith without works is dead also.

JAMES 2:24–26 NKJV

THE SCARLET CORD

Rahab the harlot was most likely informed of everything going on in her city. She was a survivor. She knew when to speak, and also when to remain silent and listen.

Rahab undoubtedly heard daily talk about the intimidating Israelites camped across the Jordan River. Surely she was already aware of the stories about how the Lord had rescued His people from the Egyptians, parted the Red Sea, and led them to safety. Since Rahab's home was built on Jericho's city walls, she may have been able to see the Israelites' activities across the river.

Rahab may have felt a tugging deep within her heart. Had the Israelite God already given these intruders the land beneath her home?

And what did she think when two strangers slipped through the city gate and came to her home?

How soon did they tell her they were Joshua's Israelite spies?

Could it be that God was encouraging her to protect the men? Rahab didn't hesitate to hide them under some neatly arranged stalks of flax she had drying on the roof. Concealing her fear, Rahab sent the king's men pursuing the spies in a false direction. Rahab saved two strangers and endangered herself and her kin by doing so.

Darkness fell. The king's searchers left. Jericho's city gate was shut for the night. But the spies never left the spot where Rahab had hidden them. When all appeared safe, she went to the roof and told them they could come out.

Conversation between Rahab and the men during those next few minutes was recorded for history:

> *"I know that the LORD has given you the land, that the terror of you has fallen on us, and that all the inhabitants of the land are fainthearted because of you.*
>
> *"For we have heard how the LORD dried up the water of the Red Sea for you when you came out of Egypt. . . . And as soon as we heard these things, our hearts melted; neither did there remain any more courage in anyone because of you, for the LORD your God, He is God in heaven above and on earth beneath."*

JOSHUA 2:9–11 NKJV

Rahab begged the men to show kindness to her and her family. The men agreed to protect them as long as she kept their identities a secret.

Rahab guided the men to a window overlooking the outside of the city wall. She looked all around to be sure no one was watching and then lowered them one at a time with a scarlet cord to the ground. She told them to hurry to a nearby mountain and hide three days, or until the search for them ended. This way, they would be able to return safely to the Israelite camp.

The men promised Rahab they would arrange for her safety. Yet there were two things she needed to do. She must take the scarlet cord used to lower the men and hang it in her window for all the Israelites to see. The strangers also ordered her to keep her family inside her home and not go out until an Israelite came for them.

Rahab solemnly promised, "According to your words, so be it" (Joshua 2:21 NKJV). She sent them away and tied the scarlet cord in the window.

Did Rahab's belief in the Israelites' true God intensify once she found out what happened when they stepped into the Jordan River? The flooding waters banked up on both sides so the Israelites could walk safely through.

Rahab waited in fearful anticipation while God's people camped only a short distance from Jericho. What would happen next?

Jericho's gates slammed shut. No one could come or go from the city. Rahab surely trembled with excitement when she heard rams' horns blowing and the marching of many feet. Around the city they went. After that, they left for their camp. All was silent. For six days, Rahab heard the rams' horns blow. The marching continued, one time around each day. Perhaps the tramping of the Israelites' feet created such a vibration that the lamps and pottery rattled

The seventh day arrived. This time the Israelites didn't stop marching after the first round. Rahab must have rechecked the scarlet cord to be sure it was in plain sight and watched out her window as the huge crowd of Israelites marched on. They tramped around the entire city six times and kept going! Tension filled the air when they circled the city a seventh time. Suddenly, there were deafening trumpet sounds and triumphant shouts.

Everything shook. Walls tumbled all around Rahab's house. Would God protect her family because of her faithfulness? No one could go outside. They could only wait.

Joshua's spies kept their word and rescued Rahab and her family. Quickly, the men led them safely outside to the Israelites' camp.

Rahab's heroism left its mark in history. Some Bible scholars say she may have left an even greater legacy by marrying an Israelite named Salmon and giving birth to Boaz. Boaz was the great-grandfather of King David, whose lineage went down through the years to include Joseph, husband of Mary, the earthly mother of Jesus.

When Rahab was confronted with a need, she didn't tarry. She did something immediately. Not only did she have faith, but she put that faith into action. Although her background was undesirable, God obviously saw something priceless in this woman.

God calls all kinds of people. Some are highly educated and come from "fine" backgrounds. Others, like Rahab, are easy to ignore. Yet they are equally valuable in His sight. Rahab is best remembered not for having been a harlot, but for being a woman willing to step out in faith in her newly found Lord and God.

No situation exists that someone hasn't faced before. God loves us right where we are. As you turn to Him and take your first step of faith, He is already there, working through your situation, transforming your life and giving you a victorious future with Him.

At times, God calls us to do something *right now.* When He does, we must act immediately and not be surprised by the wonderful miracles He has in store for us.

FUTURE

*But one thing I do: Forgetting what is
behind and straining toward what is
ahead, I press on toward the goal to win*

the prize for which God has called me
heavenward in Christ Jesus.

BUILDING THE FUTURE WITH GOD

The first Sunday Stacy and Karen Scott arrived to pastor a local church, Bob and I wouldn't have missed it for anything in the world. Stacy wore the same brush haircut and broad grin he had twenty years before. Karen looked lovely and not a year older. It was as if the couple was returning home.

Twenty years before, Stacy and Karen had served as dedicated youth pastors in the same church. They had spent countless hours spiritually nurturing our teenage sons as well as some twenty other young people. No one wanted to see them leave, but God was calling them to a different location.

Now, on their return, Stacy and Karen are able to enjoy the fruits of their past years' work. A new generation has arrived. Youth who once learned from Stacy and Karen are now adults with families of their own, filling the same pews, serving on church committees and boards, and singing to the glory of God. Church altars are filled. People are growing in the Lord!

Stacy and Karen have a gratifying opportunity once again to affect the future of the church through the present and upcoming generations.

Thank God for those who hear His call and faithfully follow year after year—touching lives, winning souls, and helping to build the future with God!

In Spite of Fear or Defeat

The things which you learned and received and heard and saw in me, these do, and the God of peace will be with you. PHILIPPIANS 4:9 NKJV

Overcoming Disappointment and Dread

Born in central Massachusetts in 1837 to a father who was a farmer and stonemason, and a hard-working mother, the seventh child in a poor family held little promise of greatness. When he was only four, his father died. His courageous mother provided for her children and struggled to keep them together in spite of adversity.

His mother's example of bravery gave the child a foundation of perseverance, as well as self-reliance. Although he earned poor grades in school, his lively ways sparked an interest in lessons learned from nature and life around him.

With little money in his pocket, he left home at seventeen and went to Boston. There he managed to sell shoes in a small store and started attending a local Sunday school.

An intense love for worshiping God was nurtured by his dedicated teacher. The Sunday school instructor saw something special growing within the teenager, something that would one day blossom into a God-given ability to win souls.

God opened a door later on by calling the young man to move to Chicago, teach Sunday school, and become a missionary to sailors. Forgetting his own needs, the man obeyed God's call. He found a new job selling shoes and rented a room in a run-down part of Chicago. At the same time, he began visiting hospitals and prisons, and he shared God's Word with crowds of homeless adults and children no one cared about. In a short time, Sunday school attendance grew to over six hundred.

Thrilled by this response, the man quit his job selling shoes so he could win souls full-time as an evangelist. He became a missionary in the Young Men's Christian Association, now known as the YMCA. When the Civil War broke out, the evangelist saw opportunity instead of dread, and he reached out to men in Camp Douglas, not far from Chicago.

He married a woman who shared his undying love for missions, and two children blessed their union. With the help of their Sunday school congregation, he built a large church for the still-growing numbers attending. A few years later, the building burned to the ground in the Great Chicago Fire.

Rather than give in to disappointment or the

dread of uncertainty, he saw the fire's tragedy as the next step of a huge opportunity God was providing. He went east and held revivals in Brooklyn, Philadelphia, and many other places. God blessed him with enough money through offerings to build a mammoth new tabernacle in place of the church destroyed by fire. Not counting adults, the Sunday school now exceeded one thousand children!

His evangelistic work continued to expand to other cities, states, and even countries. Ira Sankey joined the evangelist with glorious song as they continued winning numerous souls to the Lord.

Throughout the years, the two held some of the greatest revivals in the nineteenth century. Sunday school teacher and evangelist Dwight L. Moody and long-revered Ira D. Sankey are still remembered as dedicated soul winners who saw great opportunities to serve God.

How wonderful that a courageous mother taught her son, Dwight L. Moody, never to give in to fear or defeat. Equally wonderful is how one Sunday school teacher unselfishly cared about a poor teenage boy and inspired him to heed God's call.

God may send many opportunities your way to parent, teach, or simply share God's Word with anyone who will listen. Don't be afraid to heed His call. When you plant spiritual seeds, you never know how bountiful the harvest will be.

No Matter What

And looking at them Jesus said to them,
"With people this is impossible, but with
God all things are possible."

Matthew 19:26 nas

Making the Impossible Possible

I knew God was calling me to write a book on prayer. What I didn't know was how it would all come about until He showed me during one Sunday evening service. My husband gave a simple sermon on how God wants us to use our talents for Him. All we needed to do was pray for Him to lead us.

Bob reached into his pocket and pulled out a handful of change. He passed out a few coins to each person in our group. When Bob came to me, he gave me two quarters. I sat there in church, silently rubbing the quarters together, deep in thought. His sermon inspired me to take my talents and coins to the Lord and ask Him to show me how to follow His call.

I sent my first book proposal out to a few publishing companies and received the nicest rejection letters I thought editors could write. Although no one accepted the book, I was determined. I told God it didn't matter if I had to send out the proposal two hundred times, I would trust Him to stop it in the right place.

I decided to use those two quarters for a stamp when I sent the book proposal to Barbour Publishing Company. Needless to say, I was thrilled when Barbour accepted the book that would become *When I'm on My Knees*. Now I needed to put every ounce of my being into writing the best book I possibly could, with God's help.

All I had was an old computer that looked like it was rescued on the ark and an equally ancient printer, but I was very thankful for them. Since my computer wasn't compatible with the publishing company's, the publisher was willing to accept the book on paper. At the time, I was working two jobs but mustered the strength and wrote from the depths of my soul. With help and encouragement from my husband and family, my mentor and friend, Colleen L. Reece, and my treasured writers' group, I got to the final draft and was printing the book out. I thought I was home free.

Halfway through, my old printer tape cartridge ran out of ink. I hurried, cartridge in hand, to a local office supply store only to discover that the cartridges were no longer available.

I returned home, tears streaming down my face, as I lifted my need to God. When I shoved the cartridge back into the printer, a screw flew out! What would I do now? I knew God wanted me to send out this book, no matter what!

I felt Him coaxing me to sit back, breathe deeply, and pray. As I studied the mechanism, I suddenly realized that the tape had three colors. If

I pushed the cartridge completely down, it would print out with red ink. Necessity kicked in. I reached into my desk drawer and pulled out some heavy-duty packaging tape. Then I prayed feverishly. At the same time, I carefully pressed down the cartridge and taped it into the printer.

"God, please make it work," I whispered.

The manuscript printed out in a beautiful red. I hurried to a copy machine, made a black master, and mailed the book out.

Now I have two other quarters in a small picture frame near my desk. They remind me God does make a way for us to follow His call when we combine our talents and determination with His will.

TRUST AND OBEY

But we never can prove the delights of His
  love
Until all on the altar we lay;
For the favor He shows, for the joy He
  bestows,
Are for them who will trust and obey.

Trust and obey, for there's no other way
To be happy in Jesus, but to trust and
  obey.

JOHN H. SAMMIS, 1887

I Will Trust in You

Father, during the past, present, and future of my life I thank You for helping me be strong and of good courage. I will not fear, for You are the Lord, my God. Thank You for always being with me.

Through the ups and downs in my life, I know You never fail me. Even though I have my own ideas of how my life should go, You know what is best and will always care for me.

Yesterday is past, today is fleeting, and tomorrow is around the bend. Life is too short for me to hold onto any phase of my life and miss out on the blessings You have in store down the road.

Help me forget what is behind me and look forward without fear toward things to come. I will press toward the goals You set for me. Each time I hear You call, I will follow.

Remind me, Lord, to hold onto a positive attitude. Help me focus on whatever is just and pure. Encourage me to think about things that are lovely, honest, and encouraging. Let me look for the best in situations and people and exercise a positive outlook.

In all circumstances, I will trust in You. Each day as I follow Your leading,

I will build from the past, take advantage of the present, and look forward to the future. Because of Your goodness, I thank You for a peace that passes all understanding.

forgive

ACCEPTING GOD'S FORGIVENESS

"Come now, and let us reason together,"
Says the LORD,
"Though your sins are like scarlet,
They shall be as white as snow;
Though they are red like crimson,
They shall be as wool.
If you are willing and obedient,
You shall eat the good of the land."

ISAIAH 1:18–19 NKJV

FORGIVE ME

Dwight L. Moody told a story about his family and the miracle of forgiveness. When his oldest brother had rebelled and struck out on his own, their mother mourned for her son. Day in and day out she waited, praying for word from him or his return home.

Moody recalled how she watched and prayed each night. Each day she checked with the post office for a letter from him. The sad words from the postmaster always came back, "No letter yet, Mother."

As winter set in and the winds blew ferociously, the mother looked anxious. Moody remembered often walking up to the house and hearing his mother praying harder than ever, asking God to be with his missing brother wherever he was.

Whenever the elder son's name came up at the dinner table, all would grow silent. Would his mother ever forgive her son for such a thoughtless act?

On holidays, Dwight's mother would set a chair at the table for the absent son, trusting God to send him home one day.

Dwight's brother finally tired of wandering and made his way home. He was fearful of facing his mother after being gone so long without contacting her.

The wandering son climbed up a hillside where he could see his mother working through the window of the farmhouse. Tears filled his eyes as he viewed her sad countenance. It was clear his absence had grieved her terribly. How could he ever deserve her forgiveness?

His tears flowed as he saw his mother notice him through the window, with his long, dirty hair and attire. Before he knew it, she rose from her chair. The wayward son ran to the house and stopped. As the door flew open, he hung his head in sorrowful shame, barely meeting his mother's gaze.

"Mother," he stammered through trembling lips, "I am sorry. I shouldn't have left the way I did. I will never cross the threshold until you forgive me."

Arms flew around him and his mother wept on his shoulder.

What if the son hadn't accepted forgiveness

that day? It took courage to confess his wrong actions and beg for mercy. Instead, a family was united through humility, forgiveness, and love.

God wants to forgive us of our wrongdoings. He loves us even when we're worn to nothing and our hearts are torn from needless, wasted inroads of time. But we must confess our sins and then ask for and accept His forgiveness. When we do, we are united in the glorious family of God.

FORGIVING OTHERS AND OURSELVES

He answered: " 'Love the Lord your God with all your heart and with all your soul and with all your strength and with all your mind'; and, 'Love your neighbor as yourself.' " LUKE 10:27 NIV

LEARNING TO FORGIVE

Jan wheeled her red convertible into the hospital parking lot and rushed to the information desk. Her feet barely touched the hallway floors as she followed directions leading to the surgical waiting room. Thankful that Amanda's mother had called her, Jan greeted Amanda's parents with hugs and tears.

What had happened to Amanda? The parents explained that Amanda had been riding too fast on her motorcycle. She had lost control on a curve and flown into gravel along the roadside. The doctors said Amanda wasn't critically injured but had a badly broken leg that required surgery.

Jan squeezed her eyes tightly as tears spilled. "I could have made a difference," she sobbed. "If only we had stayed close. I don't think I can forgive myself. She could have been killed."

Jan and Amanda had been friends since kindergarten. When the girls reached their late teens, however, their friendship changed. Unfriendly competition and put-downs damaged their mutual regard for each other. Jan listened to other so-called friends gossip about Amanda. Sadly, Jan believed their vile tales. Finally, the two young women went their separate ways.

Jan thought back to when she and Amanda were dedicated Christians, active in their church youth group. Now they avoided one another and never went to church.

Amanda's mother patted Jan's hand, as though she were reading the younger woman's mind. "Jan, you and Amanda have allowed needless things to separate you. If you take it all to the Lord and then each other, things will work out."

Jan wandered down to the hospital chapel and sat in an end pew. She drew her knees up to her chin, locked her arms around her legs, and looked up to the cross in front.

"I'm sorry, Lord," she whimpered. "I haven't been putting You first in my life. I want to be closer to You. Will you forgive me?

"Please help Amanda get well, and show us how to forgive one another and restore our friendship."

Amanda's surgery was successful. She looked surprised and relieved when Jan came to visit. During the next few weeks, Jan went to see Amanda often. They shared their hurts and concerns honestly and talked for hours. They exposed and mended misunderstandings between them. They laughed and cried together. Jan and Amanda discovered they did not agree on everything, but they decided to agree to disagree and still be friends. God was teaching them how to love, forgive, and accept each other. God was also helping Jan to forgive herself.

The best day in their friendship was when the two good friends returned to church—Amanda riding in a wheelchair, Jan pushing. Jan and Amanda couldn't believe the sermon title in the church bulletin: Forgiveness.

Amanda leaned over to Jan. "We didn't just drift apart as friends," she whispered. "We drifted away from God and the church. He's been waiting for us here all along."

Jan smiled. "Let's start coming every Sunday and get on the right course."

They opened their songbooks and sang the familiar hymn, "There's a Wideness in God's Mercy."

There's a Wideness in God's Mercy

For the love of God is broader
Than the measures of man's mind;
And the heart of the Eternal
Is most wonderfully kind.

Frederick William Faber, 1854

Accepting Forgiveness from Others

So Moses cried out to the Lord, "O God, please heal her!" Numbers 12:13 NIV

Unconditional Forgiveness

Miriam certainly had her struggles as an older sister. She was the one who obeyed her mother's directions and hid in the tall grass, watching her baby brother, Moses, float precariously on the Nile River in his pitch-sealed basket. Her heart must have pounded with fear. When she saw Pharaoh's daughter rescue her brother, Miriam used quick thinking to suggest, "I know a woman who would care for the baby until he grows older."

When Moses returned to Pharaoh's palace, a few years later, how did Miriam feel as he went from infancy to prominence as the adopted son of Pharaoh's daughter?

Miriam probably felt honored when God later used her as a respected leader and a prophetess. She obviously was a caring and gracious woman who loved the Lord God. She felt great joy in leading the other women with tambourine as they danced and sang praises to God.

Moses, however, was the most important person to the Israelites. He had direct communication with God. Did Miriam wonder why her younger brother was always considered more important than she?

Miriam felt that she and her brother, Aaron, deserved as much recognition and rank. When Moses married a Cushite woman, Miriam did not approve. Jealousy took over and clouded Miriam's perspective of right and wrong. How could he marry that woman? She was soon caught up in selfish thoughts and began criticizing Moses to those around her.

Did she notice that Moses never reacted to her unkind words? Was his love so unselfish he only saw the best in her and Aaron, and was totally wrapped up in his love for God? Miriam went on gossiping and eventually won Aaron to her cause.

Soon Miriam felt God's anger kindle against her and Aaron. The Lord called Miriam, Aaron, and Moses to the tabernacle of the congregation.

The three of them went inside, wondering what God would say. The Lord descended in a pillar of cloud and appeared before them in the tabernacle doorway. He firmly commanded Miriam and

Aaron to step forward and stand before His cloud-concealed presence.

God didn't mince words when He spoke to them.

> *"Listen to my words: When a prophet of the Lord is among you, I reveal myself to him in visions, I speak to him in dreams. But this is not true of my servant Moses; he is faithful in all my house. With him I speak face to face, clearly and not in riddles; he sees the form of the Lord. Why then were you not afraid to speak against my servant Moses?"*
>
> NUMBERS 12:6–8 NIV

Surprisingly, the Lord never mentioned the humility of Moses. Neither did he discount the importance of Aaron or Miriam's role in serving Him. God made it clear, however, that He and Moses had a special relationship. He chastised the brother and sister for not showing Moses respect.

Miriam felt God's anger again when the cloud lifted and His presence left her and Aaron standing there. In an instant, her skin turned white as snow from leprosy! Her mind went numb with shock. Her ears barely heard Aaron frantically begging Moses to forgive both of them.

The Bible doesn't mention Miriam ever saying she was sorry or seeking forgiveness. Yet, Moses didn't hesitate to beseech God's mercy on behalf of the sister he loved.

Miriam had plenty of time to ponder while being shamed and shut away from the camp for seven long days. As she stared at her rotting skin, Miriam surely learned God's lesson never again to show disrespect or gossip against Moses.

How grateful she must have been when God healed her leprosy and allowed her back in camp! How thankful was her heart to receive forgiveness from the Lord and Moses!

Perhaps someone has spoken unkindly or gossiped about you. Perhaps you have done so to another. Words float through the air like dried-up fall leaves. No matter how hard we try to take them back, the tales gather momentum as they go.

The most heartening and powerful way to overcome hurt is to take the whole miserable problem to the Lord in prayer. Let us heed the lessons of Moses' forgiving spirit. Everything can change as talebearers wholeheartedly ask forgiveness from God and others. And as genuine forgiveness takes place, all becomes new.

God forgives. So can we.

MERCIFUL FORGIVENESS

Lord, I messed up again. Not only did I create stress in my own life, but I hurt You and my relationship with others.

How could I have been so uncaring and thoughtless? Please forgive me.

Hear my prayer, O Lord, for I need You more than life itself. Save me from these unkind things I have done, and be compassionate to me. I cry to You with all my heart and lift my soul to Your loving presence. Give ear to me, O Lord; hear my earnest prayers. Listen to my supplications. In this day of my trouble, I beg for Your merciful forgiveness.

Thank You for Your boundless compassion. Though I feel unworthy, You are still here wrapping Your arms around me and loving me as Your wanted child. There is no other like You, dear Lord. Your wisdom and works exceed all else. I offer myself before You as a sacrifice. I worship You and want to glorify Your name. You alone are great and mighty. You alone are my God.

Help me let go of my stubborn ways. Cleanse my heart, I pray. Renew a pure spirit within me. Please grant me direction in righting the wrongs I have done. Give me strength, dear Lord, as I seek forgiveness from others. Even if I have been right in some ways, help me to let things go. Show me how to forgive, no matter where the fault lies. Help me swallow my pride, even if others aren't willing to forgive or help to make things right.

I don't have the wisdom to straighten things out, but I know You can show me, if I listen and obey You. Instruct me, dear Lord, so I can follow Your upright ways. Unite my heart with You as I glorify Your name and praise You for Your merciful forgiveness.

Love

RECOGNIZING GOD'S LOVE

For you are the Fountain of life;
our light is from your Light.
Pour out your unfailing love
on those who know you!
Never stop giving your salvation
to those who long to do your will.

PSALM 36:9–10 TLB

ORANGE

It was early afternoon. Two of our sons and I had just arrived home from a regular day of work and school. Our youngest son, David, quickly completed his chores and homework and went out to have some fun with neighborhood friends. I started dinner simmering on the stove. Our elder son Jonathan was finishing up his homework at the dining room table.

Suddenly, David burst through the front door and ran to my side. "Mom, you really need to come help us out front."

David's tone of voice told me his request was important and couldn't wait. I quickly dried my hands, turned off the stove, and followed him out the door, with Jonathan on my heels.

I could see neighborhood kids clustered on our grass near the curb. When we reached the group, I was surprised to find the center of attention was the tiniest orange kitten I had ever seen away from its mother. It appeared to be injured. The children were trying desperately to help and had wrapped paper towels around the little creature. In spite of their efforts, the kitten shivered uncontrollably.

"What have we here?" I ventured.

David and his friends barely took their gaze from the kitty to tell me its horrible encounter. "Some big, black cat beat it up until we rescued it." One of the kids pointed to its miniature face covered with blood.

"Does it belong to anyone?" I asked.

The answer came back, a sad "No."

Sensing David and Jonathan holding their breath, my humanitarian instincts kicked in. "We'll take him in," I said. Jonathan gathered the little creature up, paper towels and all, and we took it inside.

In a matter of minutes, our family went into action. First, we said a prayer; then I grabbed a towel and handed it to Jonathan.

As I cooked dinner, my heart was warmed at the loving efforts put forth by our sons. Jonathan wrapped the shivering ball of fur in the towel and settled into our rocking chair. David knelt beside the chair, offering warm milk from his fingertip. The kitten kept shivering and didn't respond.

Jonathan snuggled it close to his chest, rocking and singing softly. Were we going lose this little creature from shock? The boys refused to give up. Finally, after two hours of continuous TLC, the kitten stopped shivering and gingerly lapped the milk from David's finger.

Pleas to keep him were met with the words, "Only until we can find another home."

It took a lot of love from the whole family and plenty of care to nurse the little orange fluff ball back to health, but we succeeded. None of us was able, of course, to find it another home. The kitten gradually won the affection of everyone in our family, including my husband Bob. Orange, the kitten would be called. That's how big it was. The size of a fluffy little orange.

Orange taught our family what compassion and tireless devotion were all about. The only way that kitten could have survived was by recognizing the help being given by two caring boys, and its being willing to accept and trust their love. Best of all was the pleasure Orange gave us as a part of our family.

God has far more love for you and me than what we were capable of giving Orange. Isn't it wonderful how the Lord constantly cares about us as He offers His love and protection! The only way we can benefit, though, is to recognize and accept His love personally.

God is with us day and night, through good times and bad, no matter where we are. His love for us is measureless.

ACCEPTING GOD'S LOVE

*"In repentance and rest is your salva-
tion, in quietness and trust is your
strength."*

ISAIAH 30:15 NIV

GOD CAN, SO CAN I

Many of us laugh at slapstick comedies on TV and
in the movies. In real life, too, such chaotic bun-
gles can still be uproariously funny. Yet when
someone commits a series of blunders, however
unintentionally, humor may turn to frustration,
pain, and, perhaps most devastating, insecurity.

After listening to people from different walks
of life share their concerns, I find insecurity is no
respecter of persons. For example, anyone can think
they are too fat, too thin, too tall, or too short. Their
hair—a common source of frustration!—can be too
straight or too curly. More seriously, one hears these
laments: "I was raised on the wrong side of the
tracks"; "My parents criticized me all the time"; "I
can't be perfect in this or that, so why try"; "I was
always told I was no good"; "I'm not talented or
smart enough."

I admire people I see who are outstanding
examples, who seem to have it all together. Yet,
when I take time to talk with them and hear their
needs, I realize many go through similar struggles

and are just as vulnerable as you and I.

Some reasons for feeling insecure are obvious. One that took me by surprise in my own life, however, was brought about by change. Emotional turmoil within me gradually began to grow. Its approach was so subtle, I didn't recognize what was happening.

After quitting a second job where I had worked for over ten years, my life was drastically changed. I was thrilled at being able to come home after teaching during the day and have time for writing in the afternoons and early evenings (instead of the hours approaching midnight). Sweet rest removed the ache from my body. Now I could catch up on house and yard work. Best of all, I was happy to enjoy evenings with my husband and family.

Instead of peace and happiness, though, the change turned every area of my life topsy-turvy. How would I handle being home more? Now that I could finally be an active part of my grandchildren's lives, would I fit in? Or would I be intruding? I was moonlighting before any of these treasured ones of mine were born. Although we've always been a close family, working long hours had forced me to miss out on a lot of little things in their lives.

The more people pressed me to fall into my new lifestyle, the more my frustration grew. I often became clumsy, dropping things and stammering for words in public. My self-esteem was hitting an all-time low.

I knew I wasn't failing God because I was doing my best. I also knew He loved me. Although His constant reassurance comforted me during that difficult time, I still couldn't get past my lack of confidence. I gradually began to avoid people who were dear to me. If I couldn't be at my best, I didn't want to be around anyone.

Thanks to the understanding love of Bob, my family, and closest friends, I began to recognize a pattern. Lack of self-worth wasn't just attacking me in one area but in every single thing I was doing. I felt I could no longer say the right things, relate properly to others, teach effectively, or even do my best writing.

When I realized what was happening, I knew there was only one thing to do. I had to face this giant lack of self-esteem head-on. Trying to bolster myself and use the old Pillsbury "white-thumb philosophy" that I could do it just didn't work. The change had to come from within me.

I recognized this wasn't the way God wanted me to be, so I asked for help from Him, my family, and close friends. I searched the Scriptures and gleaned advice from Christian "positive thinking" books. I prayed for the Lord to provide encouraging words from people around me.

Each time I felt fragile, I paused and prayed for encouragement. Then I shoved the negative thoughts from my mind and replaced them with a positive promise from God's Word:

I praise you because I am fearfully
and wonderfully made;
your works are wonderful,
I know that full well.   PSALM 139:14 NIV

God answered my prayers in the most astounding ways. Those who understood eased up on pushing me so hard in various responsibilities. And encouraging words did come. "I'm proud of you" and "You can do it" bolstered my spirits. Best of all, I felt God's assurance that He had confidence in me. The more I accepted His love, the more I felt I could be a blessing for Him. Little by little, He mended my frayed emotions and renewed my way of thinking to an "I can" attitude. Now whenever an inkling of insecurity strikes, I pull up a Scripture from my mental log and tell myself I may not be perfect, but with God's help, I can do what He wants me to do through Jesus Christ because He gives me the courage and strength I need.

Although I'm still a perfectionist in some ways, I'm learning not to be afraid of bungling. If I try and fail, at least I've done something. Never to try is never to succeed.

God helps us say, "I can!"
He fits us in *His* plan.

LOVING GOD FIRST

Do not be yoked together with unbelievers.

2 CORINTHIANS 6:14 NIV

WHOM DO YOU LOVE MOST?

Warm summer night breezes wafted from a nearby lake into the camp-meeting tent and gently wove in and out through the congregation. The sides of the tent swayed in a rhythmic pattern as seventeen-year-old Ben dreamily gazed at the sawdust chips fluttering in the aisle.

Although the evangelist's sermon seemed to lift the tent roof, Ben never heard a word. All he could think of was Patsy. Her face blocked out everything else. How he wished she were here! Ben loved the Lord, but he loved Patsy, too. He felt torn. Even though he had to admit that Patsy wasn't a Christian, he felt she would change.

After the service, Ben and his youth pastor took a walk near the lake. The moon shone brightly enough to light up the shore. Ben shared his feelings for Patsy. The young pastor listened and then looked straight into Ben's eyes.

"Do you love God more than Patsy?"

Ben gasped. "How can such a thing be possible? Wouldn't it take away from my love for her?"

The pastor shook his head and smiled. "My wife and I put God first in our marriage. This way He can lead us, and the love we have for one another grows stronger under His care.

"Ben, would you be willing to give Patsy up if God asked you? The Bible says we as Christians should only marry someone who has also accepted Christ as his or her Savior."

Ben couldn't answer. After returning home, he thought about their conversation. He knew God was talking to his heart. Gradually, Ben's love for the Lord grew stronger. He realized the love he felt for Patsy was shallow and not what God intended. Even though Ben had talked with her many times about asking Jesus into her heart, she made no attempt to do so. Not long after, Ben and Patsy drifted apart.

Four years later, Ben met a young woman at Bible college who was a dedicated Christian. After graduation, they married and entered the ministry. Ben still thanks God for his youth pastor's wise words about whom God wants us to love the most. Because he put God first, the Lord was able to guide Ben to his beloved soul mate and a life of fulfillment and joy.

WHO IS OUR FIRST LOVE?

How can we possibly love God more than our sweethearts or spouses, our children or parents? These people are more precious to us than price-less jewels. Still, this is what God calls us to do as

Christians. Does loving God more than anyone else mean we cherish our dear ones less?

Obviously, our love for one another is incredibly strong. Many a story is told about boundless acts of sacrifice shown for loved ones and even to strangers. Our entire world may be wrapped up in very special people. This love, no matter how strong, is human and sometimes fragile. Even in the best of circumstances, human love errs. Unkind words may be spoken. Thoughtless actions can cut to the heart. The fire of human love may become vulnerable enough to flicker, fade, or even die. We have heard many times of strong affection turning to intense bitterness.

How does God's love differ? It is unselfish, perfect, and pure. It doesn't manipulate or expect a payback. We can thank Him over and over that we are able to count on His care every day, in every circumstance. *God's* holy compassion cleanses us from selfishness and wrong. When we put Him first, the Lord teaches us to cherish one another *more* with a deep, unselfish, measureless love.

He cherishes us in spite of our failures and appreciates our efforts to serve and obey Him. How awesome and farseeing our Lord is! His example of pure, undefiled compassion helps us to look beyond the imperfections in others, appreciate them, and give them the love of God.

Drawing Strength from God's Love

*May the God of hope fill you with all joy
and peace as you trust in him, so that
you may overflow with hope by the
power of the Holy Spirit.*

Romans 15:13 NIV

Dark Blues and Sunshine Yellow

In the darkness of early morning, Elaina sat on a kitchen chair, hands clasped over her ears. She didn't want to hear the living room clock chime four times. Soon her newborn baby girl would awaken.

Elaina bowed her head. "This is all too much, Lord," she prayed softly. "First, I became deathly ill while carrying my baby. Then we moved from the country to the city, when I didn't want to. And now I have baby Jessica.

"I love her more than life, Lord. She and my husband and our little Matthew depend on me. But this is more than I can handle."

Elaina continued praying. "My life is out of control, Lord. I can't think clearly. I can't sleep. When I do, it's at the wrong times. I want out of all this. Sometimes I want to die. Take me home, Lord, or *please* help me."

Elaina heard slippered footsteps in the hallway. She felt her husband Jim's hand on her shoulder. He knelt beside her. She fell into his arms and sobbed.

"I can't do this anymore, Jim. I love you and our children, but everything is so dark." Elaina soaked Jim's shoulder with her tears.

Jim gently tilted her chin with his fingers. He brushed away her tears and gazed into her eyes. Elaina could feel the strength in her husband's loving hands.

"Sweetheart, I believe you're suffering from postpartum depression—baby blues. Too many things were thrown our way. But if you cave in, you have even more to lose."

Jim's voice trembled. "I love you, Elaina. You and the kids are my life. Please don't give up. We can do something."

That night at church Bible study, Elaina and Jim told the group what Elaina was going through. Several people shared how they had suffered from depression or knew someone close to them who had. Elaina was no longer carrying her huge burden alone. Her prayers were being answered. She and Jim knelt together as their friends surrounded them and prayed. The little prayer group didn't stop there. They took turns helping with meals and baby-sitting so Jim and Elaina could get away for short periods.

Elaina sought help from her doctor and counseled with her pastor. She felt God calling her to experience joy and peace. The mental fog lifted, her emotions leveled, and her body grew strong again.

Several months later, Elaina sat cross-legged

with Jessica on a blanket in a nearby park. She blew air on the baby's tummy as both of them laughed. How beautiful her little girl was!

Elaina's gaze drifted to Jim pushing Matthew on a swing. She looked above them through the trees, toward the clear blue sky.

"Thank You, my dear Lord, for lifting that terrible depression from me and changing my darkness into light," she whispered. "Help me continue to take good care of myself. Thank You for loving me and giving me so much happiness."

PUSHING OUT THE CLOUDS

Do you ever feel overwhelmed from circumstances you can no longer handle? Are anxiety and despondency flooding over you to the point where you can't sleep, and when you do, sleep comes at the wrong times? Perhaps terrible nightmares even bolt you out of bed. Do little things become huge? Are you fearful? Do you want to give up? At times, this can be a simple case of the blues. The blues can grow darker, however, and develop into depression.

We must remember how God is far greater than the most serious of our problems. He is the master healer of our bodies, emotions, and souls. God tells us to take our burdens to Him. He helps make things easier and lightens our loads when we trust in Him. Moreover, He provides us with Christian pastors, counselors, doctors, loved ones, and good friends. Don't be afraid to lean on Him and those who love you. You don't have to go through it all on your own.

God loves you. He cares, even when you are at your lowest ebb. He is your retreat, your security, and your strength. He is *always* present—in the good *and* bad. Through His power, God is calling you to push out the clouds and see clear blue skies and bright yellow sunrises. As we turn to Him, He guides us into joy and peace and hope for the future.

WHEN MORNING GILDS THE SKIES

When morning gilds the skies,
My heart awaking cries,
May Jesus Christ be praised:
Alike at work and prayer
To Jesus I repair;
May Jesus Christ be praised!

EDWARD CASWALL, TRANSLATOR

LOVING OUR MATES

So husbands ought to love their own wives as their own bodies; he who loves his wife loves himself. EPHESIANS 5:28 NKJV

An excellent wife is the crown of her husband. PROVERBS 12:4 NKJV

Forever Love

Our son Jonathan and daughter-in-law Cynthia have an abiding love for each other that will last a life-time. It gives my husband Bob and me warm feelings each time we hear them talk about one another.

Recently, Jonathan called just to say hello. He told how when Cynthia curled up near him, he discovered a gray hair in her head. They were so excited, they jerked it out and held it up to the light, marveling over its silvery sheen. Jonathan went on to share how they carefully placed the silver strand in a plastic baggie for safekeeping.

Bob and I chuckled. He warned them not to jerk out too many or she might grow bald. Jonathan continued with a timeless story I shall never forget. He visualized how beautiful his dear wife would be years from now with a head adorned in silvery gray.

He pictured how they would take walks in the moonlight, the same as they do now. In his vision, his wife's silvery hair reflected the light of the moon, their love being as strong as ever. (I believe it will be even stronger.)

The Bible says God knows every hair on our heads. Isn't it incredible that He loves us every hour of every day? It's even more incredible that His love will remain with us forever.

LOVING OUR PARENTS

And Ruth said,
    Intreat me not to leave thee,
or to return from following after thee:
for whither thou goest, I will go;
and where thou lodgest, I will lodge:
thy people shall be my people,
and thy God my God.   Ruth 1:16 kjv

FAITHFUL LOVE

After the loss of her husband, emptiness engulfed Ruth. Although she lived in Moab, Ruth had grown to love the God of her husband and her mother-in-law. Now He was her God, too.

Not only had Ruth's husband died, but so had her father-in-law and the husband of her sister-in-law, Orpah. Ruth had no one left of her new faith except her beloved mother-in-law, Naomi.

Many years ago, a famine in Judah had brought Naomi to Moab. Now that the famine was over, Naomi wanted to return to her homeland. Ruth listened as Naomi instructed her daughters-in-law:

"Go, return each to her mother's house: the LORD deal kindly with you, as ye have dealt with the dead, and with me.

"The LORD grant you that ye may find rest,

each of you in the house of her husband."

But how could Ruth remain behind? She didn't believe the way of her ancestors, nor did she worship Chemoth, their god. Ruth trusted in the one true God. She wanted to go with Naomi to Judah and begin a new life there.

Ruth threw her arms around Naomi. "Intreat me not to leave thee," she begged between sobs, "or to return from following after thee: for whither thou goest, I will go; and where thou lodgest, I will lodge: thy people shall be my people, and thy God my God:

"Where thou diest, will I die, and there will I be buried: the LORD do so to me, and more also, if ought but death part thee and me." Her heart leaped with joy when Naomi said yes.

By the time they arrived in Bethlehem, it was the beginning of the barley harvest. Ruth offered to glean from the crops so that they would have food. Not by accident, she went to a field owned by Boaz, a prosperous landowner. Little did Ruth know that God had a plan beyond her wildest dreams!

Some of the people in Bethlehem looked down on Ruth because she was from Moab. In spite of her being shunned, the loyal daughter-in-law worked hard from morning until evening, barely stopping to rest.

Ruth didn't know Boaz was asking about her, who she was and where she came from. She didn't know that when he heard of her faithfulness and care of her mother-in-law, it touched his heart.

Boaz came to Ruth one day and offered his help. "Go not to glean in another field, neither go from hence, but abide here fast by my maidens [servant girls]."

Ruth was surprised when he offered her water along with his workers. After all, she was a Gentile and a foreigner with a heathen background. She could understand his kindness to the maidens who worked for him, but the generosity he showed *her* was pure grace. He even asked her to eat with the workers at mealtime. Was it an accident that extra handfuls of barley fell in her path?

When he approached her, she bowed low to the ground. "Why have I found grace in thine eyes, that thou shouldest take knowledge of me, seeing I am a stranger?"

Boaz's voice was filled with kindness. "It hath fully been shewed me, all thou has done unto thy mother in law since the death of thine husband.

"The LORD recompense [repay] thy work, and a full reward be given thee of the LORD God of Israel, under whose wings thou art come to trust."

Ruth brought home enough barley from one day's work to feed the two women for five days. Ruth could see the surprise on Naomi's face when the older woman saw all the grain.

Naomi asked where Ruth had gleaned that day. When Ruth told her mother-in-law it was in the field of Boaz, the woman exclaimed, "Blessed be he of the LORD. The man is near of kin unto us."

One day, Naomi told Ruth that Boaz would be

staying all night on the threshing floor. He had to separate the chaff from the barley and remain there to watch over the grain.

Ruth listened as Naomi instructed her to wash and perfume herself, dress in her best garments, and go to the threshing floor.

Then Naomi warned her loved one, now called Daughter: Ruth must wait until everyone was asleep, then uncover Boaz's feet and lie down.

Naomi assured her that Boaz would know what to do.

Ruth must have trembled as she obeyed Naomi's instructions. She waited as told, then tiptoed in and curled up at Boaz's feet. In the middle of the night, Boaz awakened and discovered Ruth at his feet.

"Who art thou?" he demanded.

"I am Ruth thine handmaid [servant]," she shakily replied.

Ruth explained how her mother-in-law was a close relative of Boaz. The tradition was for a person of wealth to look after family members who were in need.

Even before Ruth and Boaz knew of the family connection, they may have already been falling in love. Had she won his admiration by the way she lived? Was she a woman worthy of his love? It appeared to be so.

Boaz told Ruth to rest at his feet until morning and leave before anyone saw her. This way no one would think wrongly of her. She would save herself until marriage. Ruth lay awake at Boaz's feet, wondering what the future held.

According to tradition, a closer relative to Naomi would have first choice at marrying Ruth. However, this man chose not to and passed this right on to Boaz.

Soon Ruth and Boaz were married. Ruth's heart must have leaped with joy again when she silently renewed the vows she had given to Naomi before leaving Moab:

Whither thou goest, I will go; and where thou lodgest, I will lodge: thy people shall be my people, and thy God my God.

God blessed Ruth and Boaz with a baby boy. They named him Obed, meaning "servant" or "worshiper." Ruth surely felt an overwhelming gladness from the love of Boaz and the mother-in-law who now valued her more than seven sons.

Little did she know the blessings would not end there. One day, Obed would have a son named Jesse, who would be father to David (later to become King David).

From a loving daughter-in-law of Gentile descent came offspring that traced through generations to Joseph, the adoptive father of Jesus.

LOVING OUR CHILDREN

"And these words which I command you today shall be in your heart. You shall teach them diligently to your children, and shall talk of them when you sit in your house, when you walk by the way, when you lie down, and when you rise up. You shall bind them as a sign on your hand, and they shall be as frontlets between your eyes. You shall write them on the doorposts of your house and on your gates." DEUTERONOMY 6:6–9 NKJV

SOWING WITH PATIENCE AND LOVE

Charles H. Spurgeon drew a practical analogy between instilling God's values in children and the centuries-old practice of planting beans. Like the tried and true method of planting beans—one bean for the worm, one for the crow, and one to survive and bring forth a crop—Spurgeon showed how first to mindfully and patiently teach a child lesson after lesson, precept upon precept. Lovingly, we are compelled to repeat the precious values by word and deed. And, like the third bean, undauntingly, we must keep setting the right examples until it would be impossible for the child to forget.

The child may disregard the first lesson. Our second good example could be stolen by the devil, like a pesky crow. But the third, accompanied by plenty of prayer and love, will hopefully take root deep down in the young one's soul and remain for eternity. How we rejoice as it finally pushes upward and returns bountiful fruit to God's glory!

Never give up patience or hope or love in training a child, no matter how difficult the task. Each youth holds the future in his or her hands.

LOVING THE FAMILY OF GOD

Be of the same mind toward one another.
Do not set your mind on high things, but
associate with the humble. Do not be
wise in your own opinion.

ROMANS 12:16 NKJV

GIFT OF HELPS

It was the end of a typical worship service. I happened to glance across the sanctuary just in time to see Jan do one more good turn for someone. How did she seem to know just the right thing to do? The answer was simple.

Jan has a way of tuning in to God's call and responding with every ounce of strength she can muster. Constantly on the lookout, she is extremely sensitive to the needs of those around her.

The most wonderful part is that Jan doesn't

appear to be interested in receiving any recognition for the things she does. She merely renders help, puts it behind her, and goes on.

Jan looks for the best in everyone she meets. When she comes to the aid of others, there are no strings attached. She doesn't want them to feel obligated, nor does she try to run their lives. She simply loves and cares. She makes no big deal but smiles as though helping and giving warms her heart.

Quiet, thoughtful acts often have a way of multiplying in value. They range from kind notes sent to someone, groceries or money given to those in need, and pinch-hitting for different church committees to slipping coloring pages and crayons to a restless child in church.

Where does she get this talent? God blesses some folks with numerous gifts of the Holy Spirit, as mentioned in 1 Corinthians 12, and upon some Christians He bestows the gift of helps. The gift of helps unselfishly uses all the productive *fruits* of God's Holy Spirit: unconditional love; overflowing joy; peace that surpasses all understanding; enduring patience; tireless kindness; unselfish goodness; faithfulness in all circumstances; empathizing gentleness; and strong, steady self-control.

How beautiful it is when someone with God's gift of helps hardly ever notices when others fail, and *forgets* his or her personal loving deeds given!

Thank you, Jan, for blessing those around you with God's gift of helps.

LOVE DIVINE, ALL LOVES EXCELLING

Jesus, Thou art all compassion,
Pure, unbounded love Thou art;
Visit us with Thy salvation;
Enter every trembling heart.

CHARLES WESLEY, 1707–1788

LET YOUR LOVE REMAIN IN ME

*Because of the love You shower upon
me, Father, I love You. Thank You for
being my dearest friend. How grateful I
am that I can talk with You about anything in my life and know You never tire
of listening. When I'm happy, You
rejoice with me. When I'm discouraged
or saddened, I feel You consoling me.
When my body is racked with pain, I
know You are here, strengthening and
healing. When I carelessly say or do the
wrong things, I experience Your correct-
ing, yet loving and forgiving, presence.*

*Teach me, in turn, to love uncondi-
tionally, under any circumstances, as
You love. If I were to possess every gift
of Your Holy Spirit, and not show love, I
would only make phony, irritating noises.
If I were able to prophesy or acquire all
the wisdom of the ages and not show*

kindness, I wouldn't be worth a penny to You or others.

If I were blessed with an abundance of faith and could see people healed and all my prayers granted and not show compassion, it would all be for naught. If I were to give all my money and earthly goods to the needy and not show empathy, my offerings would be like filthy rags. If I should be persecuted for speaking out for You and not respond with forgiveness, my words or actions would be of no substance.

Teach me love, patience, and kindness. When I feel slighted by others, Lord, I pray for graciousness to overcome any disappointment. Remind me to mix love with humility, rather than stealing the attention of others and bragging. Encourage me not to be egotistical, critical, selfish, jealous, or rude. Help me not to put other people down but to lift them up.

When someone hurts my feelings, please strongly remind me to not hold a grudge. Instead, teach me, Lord, to overlook others' faults and lift them to You in prayer for help and encouragement. Teach me to pray for the salvation of those who spitefully use me. I don't need to worry about revenge. Instead, I place it all in Your hands.

Grant me strength to be a loyal friend even when others are in the depths of sin or despair. Show me how to look beyond the problems and see their needs. Let me assure them that when they're hurting, I still believe in them and look for the best they can do. Help me to be considerate, aware that my deeds are in the best interest of my friends.

The spiritual gifts and talents You give are precious, and I thank You for them. Most of all, though, I ask for Your love, that I may pass it on to others.

I don't understand all the mysteries of life, nor do I possess tremendous intelligence or ability. I don't have answers to the world's great problems. But I can exercise Your wonderful, powerful love. When life's challenges come, I will remember that love through You conquers all. In the midst of everything we go through here on earth with its joys and sorrows, I long to see You face-to-face in all Your glorious completeness. It is then I will be able to ask You infinite questions and experience Your victorious love and joy in heaven.

Thank You for the faith, the hope,

and the tenderness You give me, Lord.
Thank You most of all for Your abiding
love. Let Your love remain in me and my
love remain in You forever.

Catch
His Vision

Visualizing through God's Word

How sweet are Your words to my taste,
Sweeter than honey to my mouth!
Through Your precepts I get understanding;
Therefore I hate every false way.

Your word is a lamp to my feet
And a light to my path.
I have sworn and confirmed
That I will keep Your righteous judgments.

Psalm 119:103–106 nkjv

A Firm Foundation

Sheldon and his wife, Evelyn, were such faithful Christians that those around them called the couple a cornerstone of their church. But Sheldon and Evelyn didn't feel that way. They believed their church was built on Jesus Christ.

There wasn't anything spectacular the couple accomplished that made folks look up to them. It was the elderly couple's rock-solid faith in God. They never wavered through good or devastating times.

Many wondered how they grew to be such strong, enduring Christians. As they listened to the stories of the elderly couple, the answers came.

When it was time to pray about needs, Sheldon and Evelyn sought the Lord in private prayer. When they went about their daily duties, the two frequently sent up silent "rocket prayers" to God. They not only prayed, but they read their Bibles, feasted on God's assuring promises, and trusted Him. When decisions had to be made, they combed the Scriptures for wisdom and guidance so they could carefully do or say the right things.

In the early years of their marriage, the couple didn't visualize how God was building a firm foundation for their lives. Prayer and Bible reading fed into their bank of spiritual strength.

When life's storms hit, they endured. When illness and stress attacked, they were able to draw from their spiritual storehouse.

From Sheldon and Evelyn, folks learned how to draw nourishment and strength from God in their own lives. Rather than waiting until a tragedy attacked and frantically begging God for help, they were learning He was already with them.

Like the foolish man who built his house on the sand, we see many who crumble under life's pressures. Heartbreak and irreparable disaster result when they do not allow God's faithful yet firm touch to prepare them to survive life in all kinds of weather.

Years have come and gone, but the strong examples of Sheldon and Evelyn, clinging to their rock, the Savior, still remain. Others have heeded their lessons. Young and old are learning to let God build their lifelong foundations with Christ and the wisdom and strength given in God's Word, the real cornerstone.

LISTENING TO GOD'S CALL

But as for me,
I trust in You, O LORD;
I say, "You are my God."
My times are in Your hand.

PSALM 31:14–15 NKJV

GOD'S WAVELENGTH

Teachers Scott and Erin decided to celebrate their first summer vacation as newlyweds by taking a two-week trip in their new camper-van. For the past ten years, Scott had been a lifeguard during summer breaks. This year, he chose to take time off so he could be with his beloved bride.

The couple, who would be traveling down the West Coast, decided not to make campsite reservations along the way. They wanted to experience life at their own pace—with one exception. Redwood National Park in northwest California was a priority, and they reserved a spot there for a specific date.

Cool July weather conditions and few traffic snarls made traveling easier than Scott and Erin had anticipated. Because of this, they reached the Redwoods two days ahead of schedule.

Scott pulled off at an empty parking lot near the ocean beach of Wilson Creek. Redwood National Park was only an hour away. Although the couple wanted to enjoy the waterfront, their main concern was finding a place to camp for the night.

Erin called the campground office on their cell phone, knowing there was little chance of getting a spot on such short notice. They hoped they wouldn't have to drive on and then backtrack. To their surprise, the ranger found a site that would be available in two hours.

Scott and Erin leisurely ate lunch and stretched out in shorts, T-shirts, and bare feet on the sandy beach. Although it was a sunny day, the weather was still a little cool. They wouldn't go surfing until it grew warmer.

Soon they were joined by a young couple who parked their car near Scott and Erin. The woman began walking the seashore while the man pulled down his surfboard and checked out the waves. Scott noticed the man was wearing surf trunks rather than a wet suit. The water must not be as cold as he thought. In any case, the young couple didn't stay long.

Right after they left, another car pulled up with a man, woman, baby, two small children, and a teenage boy and girl. The older boy and girl, clad in shorts, shirts, and tennis shoes, ran to the water and began wading. The rest of the family remained on the beach.

After about half an hour, Scott and Erin decided it was time to leave for their campsite. As they began loading their belongings into the van, Erin stopped what she was doing. She told Scott she could hear someone calling for help. They both listened and heard the call again. When they followed the sound, they could see the teenage boy and girl in the water about seventy feet from the beach. The youths were much farther out than when Scott and Erin had looked earlier.

Scott and Erin could see the boy frantically waving his hand. Once again they heard him call. It was plain to Scott that both of the teenagers were stuck in a treacherous riptide.

The teenagers' family and others frantically waved their arms, trying unsuccessfully to direct the kids to swim diagonally instead of straight ahead. No one appeared to be able to rescue the young people.

Silently, Scott instantly evaluated the situation: location, weather, winds, water. Then he pulled his surfboard off the van (cover and all) and ran toward the surf and frightened teenagers.

Erin called after him to be careful before joining the family at the water's edge. In spite of her concern for her husband's safety, Erin felt God envelop her with peace and a calm assurance. She was able to assure the parents that their children were in capable hands. She explained to them that her husband was a lifeguard and everything would be all right.

Scott knew exactly what to do as he paddled out to the young people. First, he reached the girl, who appeared to be doing all right. Scott then maneuvered his board out ten feet farther to the boy. The youth was out of breath, his eyes big with panic and fear. Scott pushed his surfboard to the boy and told him to grab onto the back and not let go, and then kick diagonally to the tide. Then Scott clutched the front of the board. The two of them paddled to the girl, where Scott gave the same instructions. Scott's calm, cheerful way helped both kids relax. Before long, they all reached shore safely.

Family and strangers gathered around the teenagers and their rescuer. Everyone surrounded Scott and Erin with hugs of relief and gratitude before the family left for their home.

Scott and Erin remained in the sun a little longer so he could warm up. All the people who had been there were now gone, and new beachcombers had arrived. The beach took on a totally different look, and all that had happened seemed like a dream. Still, the newlyweds felt God blessing them with warm feelings in their hearts. When the two later reflected on the experience, they were overwhelmed at God's timing. It was then that they broke down and cried.

Scott and Erin believe there is a reason for everything. They feel God fit several pieces together before and during their day to save two precious lives: Only God could have planned for them to be two days ahead of schedule and still be able to obtain a campsite. Only God could have planned for them to "unexpectedly" stop at Wilson Creek beach and wait two hours.

Scott and Erin's teaching experience and love for the Lord made it possible for them to be on the same wavelength as God's call and constantly tuned to needs around them. Erin was able to hear the cry for help above the roaring surf. Scott's experience as a lifeguard helped him quickly evaluate the water conditions by recalling the man surfing earlier. He knew he didn't need a wet suit, and thus he moved to the water in seconds.

Scott and Erin thank God for putting them in the right spot at the right time and helping them catch the wavelength of His call to help others.

Heeding God's Call

Then Mary said, "Behold the maid-servant of the Lord! Let it be to me according to your word." Luke 1:38 NKJV

Behold the Handmaid

On the miraculous day the angel came to Mary, she was probably occupied with daily chores, her thoughts filled with eager anticipation of her upcoming marriage to Joseph. She would give her betrothed a lifetime of happiness.

What would it be like when she became Joseph's wife and the mother of his children? She wanted to please God and Joseph in all she did.

Mary was startled when a figure appeared before her. Where did he come from? He was different from anyone she had ever seen.

The visitor was an angel called Gabriel. He told Mary, "Hail, thou that art highly favoured, the Lord is with thee: blessed art thou among women."

Fear and wonder filled Mary. Why was he saying such things to her, a simple maiden of Nazareth?

The angel spoke again, with divine authority. "Fear not, Mary: for thou hast found favour with God. And, behold, thou shalt conceive in thy womb, and bring forth a son, and shalt call his name JESUS.

"He shall be great, and shall be called the Son of the Highest: and the Lord God shall give unto him the throne of his father David:

"And he shall reign over the house of Jacob for ever; and of his kingdom there shall be no end."

A son? Mary gasped. She had saved herself for her beloved Joseph. "How shall this be," she asked, "seeing I know not a man?"

Gabriel explained. "The Holy Ghost shall come upon thee, and the power of the Highest shall overshadow thee: therefore also that holy thing which shall be born of thee shall be called the Son of God."

Gabriel went on to tell Mary that her cousin Elisabeth had also conceived and was in her sixth month. While she must have tried to suppress her surprise at this news, Mary knew Elisabeth was far too old to bear children. As if reading Mary's mind, Gabriel assured her that with God, nothing is impossible.

Because Mary knew the angel was real, and what she had been told was true, she did not hesitate before responding to consider the tremendous price she would pay. In her culture and times, unmarried women who bore children were stoned. She must heed and obey God's call, trusting Him to protect her and work out all the uncertainties.

Mary reverently bowed her head and answered, "Behold the handmaid of the Lord; be it unto me according to thy word."

The angel of the Lord left as quickly as he had appeared. Mary remained alone with her thoughts. Did she recognize the magnitude of her submission to God? When the Holy Spirit came upon her and the heart of God's Son began beating within her womb, did the Father help Mary visualize the plans He had for her, Joseph, and the child? Did she realize how God's holy design, now set into motion, would change life forever?

Consider the prophecy of Simeon the priest, whom Mary stood before with baby Jesus in her arms. "Behold, this child is set for the fall and rising again of many in Israel; and for a sign which shall be spoken against; (Yea, a sword shall pierce through thy own soul also,) that the thoughts of many hearts may be revealed" (Luke 2:34–35 KJV).

Even though Mary pondered his words in her heart, she may not have comprehended their significance.

How beautiful was Mary's response that led to the fulfillment of God's eternal plan for us all!

My soul doth magnify the Lord,
And my spirit hath rejoiced in God my
  Saviour.
For he hath regarded the low estate
  of his handmaiden:
for, behold, from henceforth all generations
  shall call me blessed.

God grant that we, too, will heed and obey His call.

RESCUE THE PERISHING

Down in the human heart, crushed by the
  tempter,
Feelings lie buried that grace can restore;
Touched by a loving heart, wakened by
  kindness,
Chords that were broken will vibrate once
  more.

Rescue the perishing, care for the dying,
Jesus is merciful, Jesus will save.

FANNY J. CROSBY, 1820–1915

LET ME SEE THROUGH YOUR EYES

Father, I get so caught up in the hurry-scurry of my activities, I often miss things You are trying to show me. I'm not always aware of the opportunities You give me to be of service to You.

Help me catch the vision of what You would have me to do. Let me see through Your eyes the needs around me. Grant me, I pray, Your sensitive Spirit. Help me to love with Your unquenchable love.

I don't know if I have the capacity to comprehend Your call for me and all it includes. I'm afraid when I see the overwhelming needs through Your eyes, it will break my heart. If I'm unable to catch all of Your vision, Lord, please be patient with me, and reveal it to me in small steps. Help me to be faithful in obeying You while we go from one point to another, together.

As You help me see things through Your eyes, I will sing of Your wonderful mercies and make Your faithfulness known to everyone You put in my pathway.

You, Father, are Lord of my all. You are my beginning and my life eternal. I give You preeminence over my mind, my heart, and my whole being.

Leave All

COMFORT ZONE

*Then Jesus said to His disciples, "If any-
one desires to come after Me, let him
deny himself, and take up his cross, and
follow Me."* MATTHEW 16:24 NKJV

LIGHTING OUR WORLD

A certain man's life story recently made the national news.

After more than twenty years as a teacher and
municipal planner, this man heard God's call to
study for the ministry. So he entered theological
seminary and began taking classes, mostly by
correspondence.

His day usually began at five in the morning
with homework and extra study, followed by his
daily school routine. After several years, he completed his academic requirements, graduated from
seminary, and was ordained a minister.

But his ministry was as different as his path to
seminary. He felt God's call to become a chaplain
for senior citizens and to preach in local churches
when pastors were absent.

His zeal and enthusiasm for life has become
an inspiration to many. In addition to his duties, he
reads voraciously, enjoys writing, and plays hymns
on his keyboard.

But what is so special about this man that

merited mention on the news? When he began his studies in seminary four years ago, he was over ninety years old! In spite of his age—or because of it—he is still obeying God's new challenges to reach souls for Christ and help light our world.

FRIENDS AND LOVED ONES

He [Jesus] told them, "The harvest is plentiful, but the workers are few. Ask the Lord of the harvest, therefore, to send out workers into his harvest field."

LUKE 10:2 NIV

RISKING ALL

The Washington, D.C., lawyer was driven to reach as many souls for the Lord as possible, and he would not be deterred. In the early 1800s, as waves of settlers descended on the Rocky Mountains, he saw his mission clearly: Many of these pioneer families needed to know about God's love.

Other Christian political leaders caught his vision and helped form an evangelical organization called Mississippi Valley Enterprise. After much commitment of work, time, money, and prayer, the association was able to send out missionaries to start Sunday schools in newly settled territories throughout the Rocky Mountains. From there,

God's messengers worked their way westward, spreading the gospel as they went.

Souls were saved and families strengthened. Slaves were freed by their owners. Sunday schools were provided for everyone, no matter their age, status, or race. During that time, more than one thousand church schools were established.

The lawyer was a loving husband and father who not only taught his children how to worship God but *showed* them through prayer and faithful example.

Along with his abilities to work legal matters, God gave the man a talent to write poetry and hymns. His compassionate songs of acclamation to God, "Lord, with Glowing Heart I'd Praise Thee," and "Before the Lord We Bow," can still be found in some hymnals today.

Years went by and the War of 1812 was well under way. Rumors spread that the British had invaded Washington and destroyed all the government buildings, including the president's home. News came that British warships were now approaching Fort McHenry near Baltimore.

Townspeople and the military scurried to get ready. Trenches were dug. Ramparts were built. One woman and her daughter worked around the clock, sewing a huge American flag. The flag must be flying over Fort McHenry before the enemy fleet arrived.

The lawyer, who had already heeded God's call in different ways, received word that his friend, Dr.

William Beanes, was being held captive on a British ship. The dedicated man was willing to risk everything, including his life, in order to rescue his friend. How he prayed there would be a way!

Before long, his prayer was answered. President James Madison gave the lawyer and Colonel John S. Skinner permission to take a boat out to the British war vessels and plead for Dr. Beanes's freedom. During the war, Dr. Beanes had shown much kindness to British prisoners. The lawyer was given letters written by prisoners, attesting to the doctor's compassion. He would show them to the British general.

The young lawyer bid his family good-bye, not knowing whether he would see them again in this lifetime. He and Colonel Skinner then boarded a small gray boat and quietly sailed toward the British fleet. At the same time, the new flag that had been quickly sewn during sleepless hours was raised. Fifteen stripes and stars shone brightly on the huge, gracefully waving banner. It could easily be seen from afar.

Two or three days later, the two brave men drew near the ships, a white flag waving above their small boat. They were astounded at what they saw. There must have been fifty to seventy warships preparing to attack Baltimore! Before they boarded the enemy ship, the two men made a pact: After they negotiated Dr. Beanes's release, all three would return to Fort McHenry and report what they saw.

When British sailors aboard the *Surprise,* the

admiral's flagship, saw the small boat with its white flag bobbing toward them, they lowered a rope ladder and the two men climbed aboard. After much discussion and reading of the letters from British prisoners, the general agreed to free Dr. Beanes. However, none of them was allowed to leave the ship until after the British attacked Fort McHenry.

The lawyer, Dr. Beanes, and Colonel Skinner paced the ship's deck and helplessly watched as the fleet approached Fort McHenry. The ships opened fire—the battle was on! Guns and cannons were fired all day and into the night.

Then everything grew silent. What was happening? When the sun began to rise, the lawyer, Francis Scott Key, strained to see. His eyes brimmed with tears as he viewed, through smoke-filled air, his country's huge flag still waving above the fort.

Mr. Key fumbled in his pocket for paper. He found an old envelope and began penning the words that swirled through his mind:

Oh, say can you see, by the dawn's early light. . . ?

Thus was "The Defense of Fort M'Henry" written, later to become known as "The Star-Spangled Banner," our national anthem.

Francis Scott Key was a man who continually heeded God's call in his life and risked everything to do so.

CHERISHED PLACES

*And Jesus said to him, "Foxes have holes
and birds of the air have nests, but the
Son of Man has nowhere to lay His
head." Then He said to another, "Follow
Me."*   LUKE 9:58–59 NKJV

FORSAKING ALL

How can we grasp the tremendous love Jesus had
for us when He obeyed His Father's call to come
to earth? Heaven, in all its splendor and glory, was
His home. There He knew no sin, no tears, and no
suffering. Then He was called to this earth, a place
in stark contrast to His heavenly home.

Certainly Jesus knew the perfect, eternal plan
and what His Father had sent Him to do. No doubt,
the Savior fully realized the suffering, pain, and
the humility of bearing our sins that He would
have to endure on our behalf. Jesus, the Son of
God, was there with His Father even before Adam
and Eve were created.

According to God's plan, Jesus obediently
came in the form of a helpless infant to a loving,
God-fearing, earthly mother and stepfather. From
the day of His birth, those who wished to destroy
Jesus searched relentlessly for the child.

While growing up, Jesus perceived things in
life far beyond His years. He must have often felt

isolated and lonely because He was different from everyone else. There were certainly times when Mary and Joseph were perplexed at Jesus' actions. The significance of the Son of God in their care went far beyond their imagination.

During His ministry, Jesus loved with an unlimited, perfect love. He felt the hurts of others, sometimes weeping Himself. He abhorred evil with a sanctified hatred. He constantly reached out and helped others, often to the point of exhaustion. And He prayed intensely for those who would follow Him.

> *Neither pray I for these alone, but for them also which shall believe on me through their word. . . . I in them, and thou in me, that they may be made perfect in one; and that the world may know that thou hast sent me, and hast loved them, as thou hast loved me. . . .*
>
> *And I have declared unto them thy name, and will declare it: that the love wherewith thou hast loved me may be in them, and I in them.*
>
> JOHN 17:20, 23, 26 KJV

Jesus left Jerusalem and crossed over the Kidron brook to the Garden of Gethsemane in order to pray. His disciples went with Him. Although He begged them to support Him in prayer, they soon disappointed him by falling asleep.

The Son of God petitioned His Father about many things during that time in the garden. He was so intense and filled with care that perspiration and tears flowed down His face. Even though the Savior dreaded the upcoming suffering and shame, He had enough love to plead for all of us.

LORD, WITH GLOWING HEART I'D PRAISE THEE

Lord, with glowing heart I'd praise Thee,
For the bliss Thy love bestows,
For the pardoning grace that saves me,
And the peace that from it flows:
Help, O God, my weak endeavor;
This dull soul to rapture raise:
Thou must light the flame, or never
Can my love be warmed to praise.

Lord, this bosom's ardent feeling
Vainly would my lips express.
Low before Thy footstool kneeling,
Deign Thy suppliant's prayer to bless:
Let Thy grace, my soul's chief treasure,
Love's pure flame within me raise;
And, since words can never measure,
Let my life show forth Thy praise.

FRANCIS SCOTT KEY, 1779–1843

HELP ME PRAY AS YOU PRAYED

Father, I hear You calling me away from my comfort and ease. I don't know if I have the ability to surrender my cherished places to You. Please help me obey Your calling, no matter the cost.

I sense You imploring me to move forward with You. In spite of my fears and uncertainties, I will glorify You in all I do, say, and think. You, Lord, have given me eternal life. Any small things I can do in return pale in Your glory.

Thank You for Your love. Thank You for dying on the cross and saving me from my sins so that I can someday be with You forever. I'm grateful for the privilege of being Your disciple.

Show me how to pray for others as You prayed for me. Grant me wisdom, Lord, as I proclaim all the good You have done for me. Give me courage to manifest Your name to everyone who will heed my words. Intervene with Your Holy Spirit and speak to the hearts of all so that they, too, will know Your marvelous love and grace.

My heart breaks when I see the sin and sickness around me. I weep over the hopelessness in so many faces. You can do miracles, Lord. The overwhelming

*part is knowing some of Your miracles
are to be done through me, Your servant.*

*I can only reach lost souls through
Your saving power and strength. I long
for people to listen to Your call, for them
to experience Your freedom from sin and
Your joy beyond measure!*

*Lord, please bless those I bring
before You at this time. I pray not only
for the ones who haven't accepted You,
but also for the loyal Christians who
struggle day after day to faithfully do
Your will. They need to be encouraged
and surrounded by Your love.*

*Strengthen my family, I pray. Gather
each one in Your glorious, protecting
arms. Touch the hearts, bodies, and
minds of my friends, and those with
whom I brush shoulders each day.*

*I pray for the same love and power
that raised Your Son, Jesus, from the
dead, to fill my life and the lives of those
around me.*

In Jesus' name, amen.

Difficult Times

Willing to Go

"You did not choose me, but I chose you and appointed you to go and bear fruit—fruit that will last. Then the Father will give you whatever you ask in my name."

JOHN 15:16 NIV

The angel of the LORD encamps around those who fear him, and he delivers them.

PSALM 34:7 NIV

Surrounded with Power

Perhaps six-foot-seven-inch former Clemson University basketball player Clarke Bynum thought of the risk when he boarded the Boeing 747-400 British Airways jet in London. He, along with the other members of a Christian mission team, were about to take off for Nairobi, Kenya.

Even though he left family and friends behind, Clarke was willing to follow God's lead. He knew there were plenty of Christians at home who would be holding him and his traveling companions up in prayer. Little did he know how much their prayers would pay off and how big the risk would be.

Clarke and the mission team were supposed to be on an earlier flight, but poor weather delayed their leaving and changed their connection to a different plane. Knowing it would be a long trip,

Clarke and his friend, Gifford Shaw, decided to take advantage of the time aboard the plane and rest as much as possible. Almost four hundred passengers were aboard the jet racing toward Nairobi.

Partway into the flight, Clarke and Gifford were jolted from their sleep when the plane made a fierce drop. It was obvious from their view out the window that they were heading straight for the ground! Needless to say, the two men believed they were about to die.

They could hear yelling and banging coming from the cockpit. Clarke knew he had to do something. As he struggled toward the front of the plane, he wondered if he would find a hijacker, armed and dangerous.

Clarke opened the cockpit door in time to see a man wrestling with the captain and copilot for the jet's controls. The plane began making a violent nosedive, then lurching upward and diving again. An engine cut out and then restarted.

Clarke lunged at the demented man, locked his arms around the man's neck, and wrestled him to the floor. The man was immediately taken into custody. Fortunately, no one was seriously injured.

After they landed safely in Nairobi, Clarke and his friend Gifford knew beyond doubt that God had helped Clarke to think and act quickly. God had given him the courage and strength to do what he had to do.

The mission team and everyone aboard the plane were surrounded with the power of prayers from Christians back home. God had kept everyone safe.

It was no accident when Clarke and the mission team were forced to take a different flight. Surely God gave Clarke a calling he never dreamed he would receive.

Grasping the Lifeline

For I am convinced that nothing can ever separate us from his love. Death can't, and life can't. The angels won't, and all the powers of hell itself cannot keep God's love away.

Our fears for today, our worries about tomorrow, or where we are—high above the sky, or in the deepest ocean— nothing will ever be able to separate us from the love of God demonstrated by our Lord Jesus Christ when he died for us.

Romans 8:38–39 TLB

A Firm Hold

Two commercial window washers evaluated the skyscraper office building windows waiting to be washed. They had started early to have enough time to complete the job.

With scaffolding and lifelines in place, the

workers followed routine procedures before ascending, including hooking lifelines to their safety belts. After cleaning supplies were loaded, they were on their way up.

But when they reached the top, something gave way. Supplies and framework plummeted toward the streets below. Lifelines snapped taut and brought both men to an abrupt stop in midair. The helpless workmen swayed precariously in the chilling wind.

Terrified, the men swung from the ropes for hours while rescue crews frantically worked to help them. Fortunately, if they lost their holds on their lifelines for even a split second, the reliable safety clamps would still hold them secure. Thank God, both men were eventually lowered to safety.

We, too, may face frightening and stressful challenges as we go out to serve God. We may have done all the right things and carefully clung close to the Lord, but something can still go wrong.

Can bad things happen even when we are obedient to God? I believe so. There is a real spiritual battle going on out there, and Satan is trying to break our Christian leaders any way He can. The devil is no gentleman. First Peter 5:8 describes how the evil one is like a roaring lion, searching for someone to devour.

No matter how tough things get, God promises He will never allow us to endure more than we can handle. When we become frazzled, brokenhearted, or weary and lose our grip, He is still there, firmly holding onto us.

God loves you and knows how much you love Him. He's there for you in the good times and disasters. He's holding tightly onto you when you soar, and when your life is crashing down. When your strength ebbs to nothing, God's powerful, firm grip takes hold. *His* strength shows up best in our weaknesses.

As you prepare to go about your routine day, be sure, above all else, to draw close to God and check out His lifeline. Then fear not! Go and serve.

In All Circumstances

Strengthen the feeble hands, steady the knees that give way; say to those with fearful hearts, "Be strong, do not fear; your God will come, he will come with vengeance; with divine retribution he will come to save you." Isaiah 35:3–4 NIV

Keep Pedaling!

Several years ago over Labor Day weekend, Stacy, our youth pastor, and Doug, a teenager, decided to take their first long-distance bike ride together. They would leave Auburn, Washington, and ride over Chinook Pass. Their goal was to reach Yakima, about

150 miles away, in one day. The following day they planned to ride another eighty miles to Kennewick, where Stacy's mother and father-in-law lived, and stay the night there.

Saturday morning at daybreak, the two riders loaded sleeping bags and backpacks onto their shoulders. Stacy had a garbage bag wrapped around his so it wouldn't get wet. They didn't know until later that if they had carried their packs lower, traveling would have been much easier. They prayed together for a safe trip and were on their way.

Pedaling uphill progressed much slower than Stacy and Doug had anticipated. They planned to have breakfast at a restaurant in Green Water, about thirty miles away. Instead, they made it in time for lunch.

Icy rain drenched Stacy and Doug's clothing and Doug's sleeping bag as they rode on. The chilled bicyclists stopped to warm up with food and hot chocolate at another restaurant near Crystal Springs Lodge, in the foothills of Crystal Mountain.

While eating, they calculated the time they were making and how far they had to go. Again, they prayed for strength and direction. Stacy and Doug knew they had to get over Chinook Pass into eastern Washington as quickly as possible. There, they hoped, the conditions would be better.

Off they pushed, logging seven steep miles to the summit of Cayuse Pass. They struggled four more miles on an even steeper grade toward Chinook Pass. Stacy thought there would be some sort of restaurant at the top where they could stop and warm up.

The closer the men came to Chinook summit, the colder the weather became. Now they were being showered with rain mixed with snow. Stacy and Doug began praying more than ever for physical and mental endurance.

Whenever they came to a stream, Stacy stopped for a drink of water. Doug, though, didn't drink as much. Partway up the mountain, Doug noticed Stacy becoming so cold that his speech was beginning to slur. This certainly wasn't the normal coherent talk of his youth pastor! The cold water Stacy had been drinking was lowering his body temperature, and hypothermia was beginning to take hold. Moreover, by now Doug's sleeping bag had soaked up so much water that it was getting heavier by the mile.

Unfortunately, when the men reached Chinook Pass, they could find no service area. How could they withstand the cold with wet clothing and only one dry sleeping bag? There was nothing they could do but keep pushing on to where the elevation was lower and where it would hopefully be warmer. The ride to the bottom of the hill would be eight more miles. There, they would come to the American River, and a campground.

Doug started out first. Because of their increased speed going downhill, the wind chill worsened. Their gloves, hats, and hair were icing over with crystalline pellets. Even though they were coasting, Doug kept pedaling to keep his blood circulating.

When they got a little ways down the pass, Doug could hear an elk off to his right in the valley. He decided to stop and listen and wait for Stacy.

When Stacy flew by Doug full speed ahead, Doug noticed Stacy was coasting but not pedaling.

"Keep your legs moving, Stacy. Keep pedaling!" shouted Doug.

Stacy couldn't hear Doug because he was riding so fast. He kept coasting as rapidly as he could safely go. Stacy wanted to conserve his energy for the next hill. Doug began pedaling and coasting again, attempting to catch up. But he wasn't able to reach Stacy until they arrived at the bottom.

Stacy steered his bike toward the campground in search of shelter just as Doug caught up with him. After crawling off his bike, Stacy collapsed to the wet, freezing ground. His cold, numb legs simply would not hold him. The two looked around them in dismay. The campground was closed. There was not a soul in sight.

Stacy finally regained the use of his legs, but both men were so chilled they could hardly move. It was plain that they were in serious trouble. To make matters worse, late afternoon was approaching and it was getting dark. Would they be able to survive such frigid conditions? Stacy and Doug walked out to the highway to seek help but no traffic came.

The men then spotted a Department of Transportation storage shed on the other side of the highway. Perhaps they could break into the shed and get temporary shelter. Stacy's sleeping bag, after all, was still dry and would cover both of them if fully unzipped.

The freezing men shuffled back to the campground and retrieved their bikes. As they were crossing the highway to the storage shed, Stacy saw headlights coming down the hill toward them.

"That's a truck!" Stacy shouted. He ran out into the middle of the road and frantically waved his arms. Stacy was right. It was a pickup truck, but it drove right past them.

Stacy and Doug gazed after the fading vehicle in disbelief. The truck went about a quarter- to a half-mile down the highway and then its brake lights flashed. The truck came to a stop. Stacy and Doug froze. The truck did not move for about a minute. Then the reverse lights came on. The pickup backed up to where the anxious bikers stood.

A man climbed from the cab and viewed Stacy and Doug sympathetically. Stacy could hardly talk, so Doug quickly explained their serious situation. The man told them he had never picked up hitchhikers, but he felt they were a pretty sad sight. The man's wife and baby were also in the cab. He told Stacy and Doug to load up their bikes and gear and climb into the back. He passed them a blanket for shelter from the wind and began driving them to a restaurant in Yakima.

Stacy and Doug discussed their situation during the two-hour drive. What would they do now? Should they check into a hospital? Spend the night in Yakima and resume their ride the next day? They finally decided to call Stacy's father-in-law to pick them up in Yakima.

A blast of what felt like hot air surrounded Stacy and Doug as they stepped through the café doors. The extreme change from cold to hot caused them to feel like they had stepped into a boiler room. The weary cyclists ordered coffee and hot chocolate. They were both so tired, they could hardly stay awake until their ride arrived.

It turned out the man who gave them a ride was from Richland. Before he left Stacy and Doug, they exchanged addresses. A couple of days later, the courageous bicyclists were able to visit the man and thank him again. Most of all, they thanked God for His protection, strength, and help.

There are times we take on projects God calls us to accomplish. We plan carefully so we can do our best job. As we prepare, however, we can't foresee uphill days or storms.

We must remember to leave unnecessary baggage behind so we don't get bogged down along the way. Drinking from God's living water (His Word) is calming and strengthening, but more is required of us. *In addition to praying and reading our Bibles, we must also keep "pedaling" for the Lord. God often provides us with an incredible passion to hold onto the vision He has given us.* By doing these things, God pumps the powerful juices of His Holy Spirit through us day after day, giving us direction, strength, and courage. We *must* run (or pedal) the race our Lord has set before us and not give up.

The next time you are worn, discouraged, and weary in the race of serving God, pause to pray and read your Bible. Then keep on keeping on for Him. Know for certain God won't leave you. He will be there to help you every step and every mile along the way.

TAPPING INTO GOD'S POWER

"Not by might nor by power, but by My Spirit," says the LORD of hosts.

ZECHARIAH 4:6 NKJV

POWER TO SERVE

D. L. Moody told of an elderly minister he met who complained of having heart problems. Concerned about his health, the senior minister decided he could preach only once a week. He asked a younger man to do any extra speaking and take over visiting in homes and hospitals.

The older minister heard a short time after about God's anointing power. If only he could preach the gospel just once with the power of the Holy Spirit before he died! He earnestly prayed for God to anoint and fill him.

The next time Reverend Moody talked with the minister, the older man's demeanor had completely changed. Empowered by the Holy Spirit, the minister was preaching at least eight times a week and leading people to Christ!

Moody believed most Christian workers do not break down from hard work. Even as machinery breaks without lubrication, Christian leaders give way under the load by working without the ongoing anointing of God's power.

I believe when things get tough, God wants us (no matter how young or old) to wait on Him in sincere prayer until we receive His power from on high.

We can then move forward, not in our own might or will, but by the continual unlimited anointing of strength and direction from God.

TIME-OUT WITH GOD

Likewise the Spirit also helps in our weaknesses. For we do not know what we should pray for as we ought, but the Spirit Himself makes intercession for us with groanings which cannot be uttered.

Now He who searches the hearts knows what the mind of the Spirit is, because He makes intercession for the saints according to the will of God.

ROMANS 8:26–27 NKJV

Greg and Myrna lived in a happy Christian home filled with teenagers. All were active in the church, with Greg leading singing and serving on the church board and Myrna teaching church school.

As time went on, things changed. Their children chose different standards for themselves, and God no longer remained their priority or interest. The teenagers were making decisions in their lives that could be disastrous.

Friction replaced joy in their home. Greg and Myrna struggled to work things out but couldn't keep afloat. How could they be Christian leaders when things weren't right at home?

The brokenhearted couple came to the Lord for direction. Because they wanted to put more love and energy into their children, Greg and Myrna both cut back on their church responsibilities. But doing less in the church was a big adjustment. A wise Christian friend sensed their need and wrote the following letter:

> *Dear Greg and Myrna,*
> *I have been praying for you today and felt God lead me to share some lessons I learned while we were raising our teenagers.*
> *First, you are doing the right thing by obeying God as He calls you apart. This is the time to focus your whole*

hearts and souls on your children. They are your most precious commodities.

Second, raising a family isn't always a bed of roses. When we brought these children into this world, they came with their own minds and wills.

Third, you are not alone. Sometimes we as Christians try to appear happy-go-lucky to one another rather than sharing our needs. Some people may turn their backs on you, but you really do have friends who love you and care. A few of us walked this road before you.

Fourth, when the struggles hit close to home, keep loving, forgiving, and praying. Cling tightly to Jesus, the blessed vine. He is your source of nourishment and strength. When you are discouraged, God will truly hold you up.

Fifth, the more you pray and keep loving, the stronger you will become. God will teach you some wonderful lessons through this. The only way you make it through is by spending earnest time in your prayer closet.

Sixth, thank God for your kids every day. When they do the smallest good things, tell them you are proud of them, that you love and appreciate them. Forgive them when they mess up. Try to love, understand, and accept them right

where they are. Look for their strengths.
Tell them you believe in them and know
they will become fine Christian adults.
Never fear, God is right there with them.
  Seventh, after you make it through
the crisis, you will all look back and
thank God for the miracles! When the
victories are won, remember to pass on
your love and blessings to other parents.
  I love you all and am here for you,
                                    Marlene

Greg and Myrna made their share of mistakes along the way, but they kept loving and praying for their children.

And God did perform miracles. Now the entire family thanks God for how He brought them through the tough times. Every one of Greg and Myrna's children loves the Lord and is a responsible adult.

The Christian couple is grateful to God that He called them apart to focus on the ones most important to them, their own family. Now they have the chance to help others and share the lessons they learned.

THANK YOU FOR LOVING MY CHILDREN

Father, these are frightening times for
me, but I trust my children to Your care.

Thank You for loving and helping them.

Grant me patience to love, wisdom to understand, and grace to accept them. I know You are watching over them, so I will not fear. I believe in my children because I see the good in them.

Thank You for calling me apart and guiding me through. I already praise You for answered prayers to come.

In Jesus' name, amen.

WINNING THE BATTLES

Finally, be strong in the Lord and in his mighty power. Put on the full armor of God so that you can take your stand against the devil's schemes. For our struggle is not against flesh and blood, but against the rulers, against the authorities, against the powers of this dark world and against the spiritual forces of evil in the heavenly realms.

Therefore put on the full armor of God, so that when the day of evil comes, you may be able to stand your ground, and after you have done everything, to stand. EPHESIANS 6:10–13 NIV

Imagine the tremendous changes the apostle Paul faced during his years of serving God. Picture how he felt as he traveled from place to place, proclaiming Christ's love. Try to understand the stress he went through in debating with prominent challengers. Think of his time in prison, where he wrote letters to the churches he had once visited.

The amazing thing about Paul is that he didn't seem to harbor bitterness toward anyone, no matter how poorly he was treated. He was no stranger to the anxiety, sadness, and pain caused by sin.

Paul shared some wonderful news with us. His battles were not against flesh and blood but against evil and the rulers of darkness. Only with God's help could he contend with such things.

In spite of the bad we see around us, there is a lot of good going on in this world. We may have to search for it, but it is there.

I love hearing the statement made by a news reporter on a local Christian radio station after he completes the report: "And now," he happily proclaims, "it's time for the good news." He goes on to share some uplifting current blessings, capped off with an encouraging Scripture.

The daily battles we face can't be successfully won on our own. We are only able to experience victories by claiming the good news in the Bible. Through Jesus, we can be free from sin. The struggles in this worrisome world aren't ours; they are a conflict between good and evil.

The Bible explains how God provides us with armor to help protect us from the wrongdoing and temptation we are compelled to face. There are no quick fixes, however. In order to see victory, we must go to God in sincere prayer about our problems, and search His Word for wisdom and strength.

God provides solutions in His Word, represented by putting on the full armor of God.

- *Belt of truth*. God wants us to be totally truthful in all things. Jesus is the way, the truth, and the life. When we know Him as our Savior, we know the truth, and the truth sets us free.

- *Breastplate of righteousness*. We can call upon the power of God's Holy Spirit to fend off temptation. He gives us the ability to recognize right from wrong, be obedient to Him, and stand firm within His will.

- *Shoes of the gospel of peace*. The word "gospel" means good news. God wants us to tell our friends and loved ones the good things He does for us. His Holy Spirit reinforces our words, and He speaks to the hearts of others. When frustration and wrong deeds surround us, He helps us respond with kindness and love.

Through soft answers, anger can often be averted.

* *Shield of faith.* Our Lord uses the tiniest shred of faith we can muster and makes it multiply. His power isn't measured by how strong *we* are. Instead, when we simply place our trust in Him, God has a mighty way of warding off the evil attacks on our lives. When He does, watch the miracles happen!

* *Helmet of salvation.* When we know Jesus as our Savior, we are absolutely confident that He keeps us as His sons and daughters now and through eternity. As we focus on Him with all our hearts and minds, He assures us of hope for today, tomorrow, and forever.

* *Sword of the Spirit.* The sword of the Spirit is the Bible, which contains marvelous answers for our lives. When we are in doubt, the Scriptures cut through the deception of evil falsehoods and show us the right way to go.

Putting on God's armor isn't some magic trick. By obeying the timeless lessons God has for us in His Word, we can live victorious, joy-filled lives *above* the circumstances.

BE STRONG IN THE LORD

"Be strong in the Lord
And the power of His might!"
For His promises shall never, never fail;
He will hold thy right hand,
while battling for the right,
Trusting Him thou shalt forevermore prevail.

EL NATHAN, LATE 1800s

MY BATTLES BELONG TO YOU

*Father God, this looks like it will be a
challenging day, but I still must put forth
my best for You. I don't know what will
happen, so I turn to You for guidance
and help. Grant me strength and wisdom
to do and say what is acceptable in Your
sight.*

*Thank You for giving me stamina
through Your mighty power. I read Your
Word and feel dressed in Your sturdy
armor—not as a gimmick, but by obeying
the lessons You teach me in Your Word.*

*I'm grateful that the spiritual battles
I face are not mine. They are Yours, Lord
God—battles between You and the evil
one. No matter the circumstances, I will
not shrink in fear. I shall not despair and
faint. For You are with me, ready to fight*

in my stead.

Help me not to crumble under the circumstances but to triumph over them. Grant me the endurance to stand firm for what is pure and right in Your eyes.

I place my hurts and fears, my actions and attitudes, in Your hands. I lift my petitions to You in prayer. I trust You to manage each one according to Your will. Lord, I thank You and praise You already for answers to prayers and victories to come!

Someday, Lord, I want to be able to say like Paul, "I have fought the good fight, I have finished the race, I have kept the faith. Now there is in store for me the crown of righteousness, which the Lord, the righteous Judge, will award to me on that day—and not only to me, but also to all who have longed for his appearing" (2 Timothy 4:7–8 NIV).

Faithfulness

KNOWING GOD'S FAITHFULNESS

God is our refuge and strength,
an ever-present help in trouble.
Therefore we will not fear,
though the earth give way
and the mountains fall into the heart of
*   the sea,*
though its waters roar and foam
and the mountains quake with their surging.
Selah   PSALM 46:1–3 NIV

LOUD AND CLEAR

I thought February 28, 2001, would be like any other day teaching first and second graders. That is, except for one thing. I was expecting an important phone call from Paul, a publishing company editorial director, and twelve sales representatives. They would be interviewing me about my books. The call was scheduled to come into the faculty room phone booth during my lunch break, at 11:20 A.M. PST, to be precise. Wendy, the teacher I assist, and I had worked out the details ahead of time so I could easily slip down the hall.

Language arts lessons with my small group around the table ran in a smooth sequence. Every once in awhile, however, I found myself glancing at the clock. Now it was 10:50, only a half hour to go.

An abrupt sound like something hitting the side

of the school building jolted us from our work.

"Earthquake!" I tried to sound calm, but the words came out as a shout.

"Everyone under the tables," Wendy ordered.

The students responded immediately. We had gone through the drill many times and were pleased to see the children do exactly as they had been taught.

For fifteen to thirty seconds, everything violently heaved and rolled, not letting up. Wendy and I knew the longer the quake, the more serious the outcome. Quiet whimpers and anxious whispers came from the children.

I tried to hold them close with one arm, like a hen gathering her chicks, and hold onto the table leg with my other hand. I didn't want to lose hold of the worktable as it was our primary shelter from possible falling debris.

Of course, it didn't take long for me to pray about our frightening situation. "God, keep these children safe and watch over my family," I urgently whispered.

My students nestling near me didn't seem to be aware of my almost-silent prayer. They already knew by our everyday examples that both Wendy and I loved the Lord.

After almost a minute, the shaking began to slow down. The room, though, felt like a huge, sloshy water bed. One little boy in my group acted more frightened than the others. His little body shook as he leaned against me.

"Shane, do you want me to hug you?"

"Yes," he squeaked.

I let go of the table leg and wrapped both arms around him and the others in my group as the tremors finally began to subside. "It's going to be all right," I assured them.

We were to remain under the table until the all-clear announcement blared from the classroom speaker, a length of time that seemed endless. Finally, the message came through, and we crawled out from under the furniture. After the initial shock, everyone went into action, checking on the safety of our children and the structure of the building. Thank God, no injuries were reported, and there appeared to be no significant damage to the building.

I glanced once again at the clock. It was 11:15. I attempted to phone a family member with no success. Then I tried calling the publishing company's 800-number to warn them about the phone lines. Still no success. I knew it would be a miracle if Paul's phone call made it through.

I hurried to the school office where the phones were ringing off the hooks. When I asked Tami if she had received the call, I couldn't believe what I was saying. *What a silly question,* I thought. How could it be possible?

Tami had one receiver held to her ear and frantically pointed to another phone. "Line one," she announced.

"I can't believe it!" I exclaimed. I hurried to the faculty room and found the surprisingly vacant phone booth. I shut the door and picked up the receiver.

"This is Anita. Paul, is that you? Yes, I can hear you." I sighed with relief. "You're coming in loud and clear. We just had an earthquake here. Yes, we're all right but a bit shaken up."

The interview went well. The Spirit of the Lord Jesus Christ vibrated through the lines during the next fifteen minutes as we talked.

I thought of the editor and sales team that evening as the national news covered extensive damage in our area and for miles around. I felt sure the company's team was also watching and keeping us in their prayers. For that, I felt grateful.

God taught me a lesson that day. No matter what kind of chaos, danger, or uncertainty is going on, our Lord is still right by our side. I believe He's wrapping His arms around us and assuring us of His love and care.

More miraculous than the editor's phone call is the way God cuts through obstructions in our world. No matter what, He still makes it possible for us to hear His call. Loud and clear.

COMMITTING TO OUR CALL

Then the LORD. . .said to him: . . . "If My people who are called by My name will humble themselves, and pray and seek My face, and turn from their wicked

ways, then I will hear from heaven, and
will forgive their sin and heal their
land."   2 Chronicles 7:12, 14 nkjv

A Call to Keep

Some time ago, Jim and Elisabeth Elliot obeyed
God's call to serve in Ecuador as missionaries to the
Auca Indians. One day while Elisabeth, her friend
Rachel, and other missionary women remained in
the village, Jim and the men from the missionary
team continued their work in the jungle reaching
out to the Auca tribe. Some of the tribe didn't understand the Christian workers' motives and were
frightened. Because of this, Jim and the other men
were tragically murdered.

It would have been easy for Elisabeth and
Rachel to give up and return brokenhearted to the
United States. Instead, they remembered God's call.
It was one not only to their husbands but to them as
well: to win the Auca Indians for Christ. Elisabeth
and Rachel weighed their promises to follow God's
call, no matter how difficult. After a stay in the
United States, the two widows felt God wanted
them to return to the Auca village and carry on the
work already begun. Elisabeth's young daughter,
Valerie, and other family members joined them.

The love and forgiveness Elisabeth, Rachel,
and others felt for the Aucas could only have come
straight from God. Because they were faithful to

what He wanted them to do, God blessed them abundantly. Numerous souls turned to God and many lives were changed. In time, some of the same men who had killed Jim Elliot and the other missionaries became Christian leaders in the church and soul winners for God.

Perhaps God is calling you to a mission field—in our country or another land, your city or another locale, to your next-door neighbor or your own household. As we humble ourselves and faithfully call upon His name, He will hear our prayers. As we earnestly plead for the precious souls He places before us, we shall hear from heaven.

Step by step, prayer by prayer, one selfless deed after another, and He truly will heal those in our land who turn to Him.

Think of it. Our commitment to God's callings can change lives and make the difference through generations for thousands of years! Nothing is impossible with Him.

God has a way of taking our miniature *movements of obedience and magnifying them into marvelous, never-ending miracles.*

WILLING TO BE FAITHFUL

And she vowed a vow, and said, O LORD of hosts, if thou wilt indeed look on the affliction of thine handmaid, and remember me, and not forget thine handmaid, but wilt give unto thine handmaid a man child, then I will give him unto the LORD all the days of his life, and there shall no razor come upon his head.

1 SAMUEL 1:11 KJV

KEEPING THE PROMISE

Imagine the despair Hannah felt at not being able to give her husband a child. How she longed for God to open her womb and allow her to give birth to a baby, especially a boy! More than anything, she desired to bestow the honor richly deserved on her husband, Elkanah.

Hannah knew Elkanah truly loved her. He often told her, and he also showed his love by giving her generous portions of the yearly sacrifice—much more than what he gave his second wife, Peninnah. Yet Hannah's heart ached whenever she watched the joy Peninnah's children brought to Elkanah. Why must the other woman torment her and cause her to weep simply because she was childless?

Hannah felt bitterness and desperation creep into her soul. Grief engulfed her entire being. She didn't want to eat. All she could do was weep.

One day, Hannah went to the house of the Lord and took her bitterness, pain, and hopelessness to Him in prayer. No matter how much she wanted a child, she would be faithful to God.

What could she give Him in return for such a long-prayed-for gift? Hannah knew it must be that which she treasured the most.

Hannah's trembling lips whispered her faithful promise between her sobs. No one could hear except her God. She prayed, "O LORD of hosts, if thou wilt indeed look on the affliction of thine handmaid, and remember me, and not forget thine handmaid, but wilt give unto thine handmaid a man child, then I will give him unto the LORD all the days of his life, and there shall no razor come upon his head."

Hannah looked up from her prayer and saw Eli the priest approaching her. She was shocked when Eli sharply accused her of being drunk! She would never do such a thing and displease God.

She quickly explained she was not drunk but was pouring out her soul before the Lord.

Eli discerned Hannah's faithful heart. "Go in peace," he proclaimed. "The God of Israel grant thee thy petition that thou hast asked of him."

Hannah gratefully responded to Eli's blessing: "Let thine handmaid find grace in thy sight."

From that moment on, Hannah surely believed God was answering her prayer for a child. Now she could eat. God had replaced her grief with hope, her bitterness with gratefulness, and her sadness with joy. She would weep no more.

The Lord did answer Hannah's prayer. He gave her a son, whose name would be Samuel, because she had asked for him from the Lord. Hannah and her husband were overjoyed and thankful to God for His gift.

It would have been tempting for Hannah to "forget" the promise she made to her Lord. Instead, she immediately prepared for the time she would return her precious gift to Him. She would keep Samuel with her until he was weaned and then take him to the temple, present him to God, and place him in Eli's care.

The time came all too soon. Hannah made the trip to Shiloh and brought young Samuel to the house of the Lord. God must have filled her with comfort and strength as she presented her only child to Eli.

"Oh my lord," Hannah said, "as thy soul liveth, my lord, I am the woman that stood by thee here, praying unto the LORD.

"For this child I prayed; and the LORD hath given me my petition which I asked of him: Therefore also I have lent him to the LORD; as long as he liveth he shall be lent to the LORD."

Joy filled Hannah's heart. She praised God and worshiped Him for His mighty love. "My heart rejoiceth in the LORD. . . . There is none holy as the LORD: for there is none beside thee: neither is there any rock like our God."

After Hannah faithfully fulfilled her promise to God, He abundantly blessed her and Elkanah with three more sons and two daughters.

The amazing blessings didn't stop there. Because of Hannah's obedience to God, Samuel became the Lord's faithful servant. Although she missed being able to raise him, she surely felt great joy, knowing he was growing in the Lord.

Not only was Hannah blessed, but so were all the people of Israel, from Dan to Beersheba. They were able to have Samuel as a prophet from the Lord. All of this came to pass because of one mother who faithfully kept her promise to the Lord.

HE GIVETH MORE GRACE

He giveth more grace
When the burdens grow greater;
He sendeth more strength
When the labors increase.
To added affliction
He addeth His mercy;
To multiplied trials,
His multiplied peace.

His love has no limit;
His grace has no measure;
His power has no boundary known unto men.
For out of His infinite riches in Jesus,
He giveth, and giveth, and giveth again!

ANNIE JOHNSON FLINT (1862–1932)

My Hope Is in Your Faithfulness

Lord, I thank You for Your unfailing faithfulness. Because of Your kindness, I know I shall never be consumed. Because of Your compassion, I know I shall never be alone. Because of Your mercy, I shall always have hope.

Every day as I quietly wait for Your direction, You shed new mercies on me. Every night, You give me portions of Your everlasting peace and joy.

Thank You, Lord, for always being with me. You are the solid rock on which I stand!

Give
and Share

ACCEPTING GOD'S BLESSINGS

*"And do not set your heart on what you
will eat or drink; do not worry about it.
For the pagan world runs after all such
things, and your Father knows that you
need them. But seek his kingdom, and
these things will be given to you as well."*

LUKE 12:29–31 NIV

FROM WORRY TO WORSHIP

How can our minds grasp all the issues we are
concerned about? From earthquakes, floods, and
tornadoes to poverty, war, illness, and death, the
list goes on and on.

We worry and speculate, but it seems to do us
little good. Although we need to be responsible for
our families and world problems, we must recognize *we* are not in control. *God is.*

Things may not always turn out the way we
want. Our prayers may even appear to go unanswered. When we wonder why circumstances happen the way they do, we must remember that God
truly loves us and cares about our every need,
whether small or large.

Later, we can look back and see the hand of
God moving in ways we never dreamed. We are
often amazed at how He saw the bigger picture,
when we were only able to perceive one tiny dot.

When fear, uncertainty, and anxiety flood over you, ask God to wipe away the worry and replace it with openhearted worship to Him. He has a magnificent way of faithfully fitting everything together for good, and bountifully blessing us when we place our trust in Him.

This can be a difficult step to take when life is really tough. Just as when we took our first steps holding a parent's hand; so when we appear pretty wobbly, God is always with us, ready to hold our hands and give us balance. We don't have to attempt these steps all at once. One tiny step of faith. One tiny phrase spoken in worship to Him.

When life crashes down on me, as it sometimes does, I look back on the many blessings God has given me. I think especially of the most fearful, uncertain experiences and how He brought me through in such miraculous ways. Then I try to mentally take the problems and place them in my clenched fist. I shakily open my palm, lay my concerns before the Lord, and ask Him to do whatever He wants with them. I pray for faith—I don't try to dictate my will for the outcome or timing. Then I say seven little words:

"Your will be done, Lord, not mine."

Once is not enough. Often, I need to pray these words for my own sake again and again. As time goes on, I experience His assuring presence. I begin to recognize His loving faithfulness at work in my life.

We may feel unworthy to receive God's awesome blessings. Do we even deserve them? The answer is that Jesus paid the price for our sins. *He* is the One who makes the blessings possible.

- Trust completely in God.
- Accept His bountiful blessings.
- Be thankful.

WILLING TO GIVE

"Give, and it will be given to you. A good measure, pressed down, shaken together and running over, will be poured into your lap. For with the measure you use, it will be measured to you." LUKE 6:38 NIV

GOD IS THE CHAIRMAN

He was born in Richford, Vermont, and later moved West with his family, attending elementary school in Portland, Oregon. When he grew older, he took courses in algebra, geometry, and mechanical engineering from a correspondence school.

Because finances were tight during his teenage years, he went to work in a garage as an iron molder and grease monkey. All the while, he continued going to school.

It didn't take long for him to want more out of

life, so he borrowed forty-five hundred dollars and started his own garage.

Hard work, determination, and natural ability, along with learning new methods at a navy yard, helped him improve in the machinist trade. By the time World War I rolled around, his creative mind had helped him produce a power-controlled unit that did a complete job of loading, hauling, dumping, and spreading, using rubber-tired wheels.

During World War II, his caterpillar-type tractors pioneered road-building equipment and provided about three-quarters of the supplies used by the U.S. Armed Forces. Some of his most helpful implements were jungle tree crushers and mechanical mules for towing ships.

His company continued manufacturing newer and better heavy machinery. His road scrapers and a wide variety of machines caused his products to be so valuable that he sold most of them to the Westinghouse Air Brake Company for $31 million.

He later designed an offshore drilling platform and came up with additional electrical ideas for locomotives and the electric wheel system.

Best of all, he was a dedicated Christian and lay preacher in his church denomination. He often explained to others how his success was due to his partnership with God, and that the Lord was the chairman of his board of directors. Everywhere he went, Robert Gilmour LeTourneau consistently demonstrated the ways he applied Christian principles to running his business.

Possessing money wasn't important to him. Instead, he lived on 10 percent of his income and gave the other 90 percent, along with portions of his company's stock, to start two large missionary stations in Liberia. He also established the LeTourneau Foundation to help fund students preparing to enter the mission field.

Another man spent his early years moving from Virginia to Kentucky to Missouri as a Baptist pastor's son. His father received no salary for preaching but made a modest income as a farmer. Although the boy's father didn't possess much, he was rich in vision. At one point he was a Populist candidate for the Missouri House of Representatives.

When the boy turned eight, his father told him he must find a means to buy his own shoes. Somehow the child earned the money and bought a pair of brogans with buckles and eyelets. The youngster soon decided to make money work for him. He immediately began saving his meager earnings and bought a pig for $2.50. After he sold that pig, he invested in more pigs and continued the process.

When he neared adulthood, he obtained a job with a leading town merchant. After graduating from Hamilton High School, he began a career as a clerk in a dry-goods store. Following some trials and failures in starting his own meat and bakery business, he met a man named T. M. Callahan.

Mr. Callahan changed the young man's life by teaching him how to successfully run a business. In time, the young man was able to purchase one-third partnership in Mr. Callahan's company. And Johnson and Callahan stores began to sprout up throughout the middle and northern states.

Before long, he was able to form his own corporation. Again, the stores multiplied. He gave his managers stock in the company, depending upon the profits they brought in from their stores. As years passed, his assets multiplied by the thousands, and then millions.

More important than this man's business accomplishments was his total commitment to God's will. James Cash Penney used his talent and made money through his J.C. Penney stores. He contributed tremendous amounts of time and money to Christian endeavors. He not only gave funds to help youth but the elderly and farming industry as well.

God blesses us with a variety of talents. Perhaps you can sing, write or tell stories, preach, perform in Christian plays, build houses, repair the plumbing for someone, or pray and give hugs. One talent is a God-given ability to make money multiply. Along with our other skills, God can use this one to reach souls for Christ and help the needy.

The Bible doesn't say money is the root of evil. Instead, God's Word says, "For the love of money is a root of all kinds of evil" (1 Timothy 6:10 NIV).

We must allow nothing to come before God. All our time, talents, treasures, and money ultimately come from Him and belong to Him. As we recognize our capabilities, let us pray for wisdom and unselfish love, and use our talents to help others and glorify the One who gives us all.

Perhaps God is calling you to use your earnings for Him. Don't be afraid to stretch beyond what you normally offer Him. Pray about it. God has a plan for you. As you seek His direction and give what He asks, He will bless you. Incredibly, we can never "outgive" the Lord.

GIVING ALL

And He [Jesus] looked up and saw the rich putting their gifts into the treasury, and He saw also a certain poor widow putting in two mites. So He said, "Truly I say to you that this poor widow has put in more than all; for all these out of their abundance have put in offerings for God, but she out of her poverty put in all the livelihood that she had." LUKE 21:1–4 NKJV

A GIFT FROM THE HEART

Proud teachers dressed in exquisite flowing robes gathered in the temple to debate religious theologies and pray lengthy prayers. As they did, rich people thronged to the temple treasury and haughtily threw in grand offerings from their abundance, attempting to gain everyone's notice.

Unnoticed amid the colorful spectacle, a poor widow stood at the edge of the crowd. She wanted to please God. Could she honor Him with her meager gift? She probably wondered if her small amount would even matter. Still, she would be faithful.

The woman edged her way toward the temple treasury. Hopefully, no one would pay any attention to her. Then she noticed a man who sat nearby. Unlike the others, He didn't seem critical when He looked up at her. What was so special about Him?

The widow held two small copper coins in her hand. They were everything she had. The coins were worth only a fraction of one of our pennies.

As the widow dropped her offering into the treasury and turned to leave, she may well have felt blessed by God's love. She had no idea, however, that her humble gift from the heart would be remembered throughout the ages.

Did she overhear and rejoice at the Master's words when He called His followers' attention to her sacrificial gift?

*And he called unto him his disciples, and
saith unto them, Verily I say unto you,
That this poor widow hath cast more in,
than all they which have cast into the
treasury: for all they did cast in of their
abundance; but she of her want did cast
in all that she had, even all her living.*
MARK 12:43–44 KJV

Even if she didn't hear the Lord's tribute, she surely received her reward from her heavenly Father, "pressed down, shaken together, and running over."

No longer is Jesus seated by the temple treasury. Now He is seated on His heavenly throne at the right hand of His Father. In the same way the Lord was pleased with the widow giving her entire living that day, He still acknowledges when we, too, give our all.

God must be pleased when we present to Him true, selfless gifts from our hearts.

GIVE OF YOUR BEST TO THE MASTER

Give of your best to the Master;
Naught else is worthy His love;
He gave Himself for your ransom,
Gave up His glory above:

Laid down His life without murmur,
You from sin's ruin to save.
Give Him your heart's adoration,
Give Him the best that you have.

HOWARD B. GROSE (1851–1939)

I will trust in You, O God, with all my heart as You direct me to give unto You. When things are tight financially, I will lean on Your understanding of how my needs will be met. Help me, O Lord, to do so, rather than trying to work it all out on my own.

I will honor You, my Lord, with all I possess. Even when it is hard, I will first give You a portion of my earnings. In turn, I know You will care for me.

Today I bring my offering to Your house of worship and give back what You have already given to me. I don't do this expecting something in return. Instead, I want to wholeheartedly give You my all.

I can't comprehend the way You sent Your Son, Jesus, from riches in heaven to our earth. Thank You for sacrificing Him and making it possible for me to become Your child. Thank You for times past when You rewarded my faithfulness with bountiful blessings, pressed down, shaken together, and running over. I'm grateful for the privilege of returning these blessings to You.

Help me to be wise with the provisions You give me. Grant me continual faith as I invest bountiful seeds in reaching others for You. Let me give from the depths of a loving heart. I pray that I may be able to see some of the glorious harvest of souls set free from sin. What greater reward could I ever receive than this! In Jesus' name, amen.

Witness
and Serve

Stepping Out on Faith

And immediately Jesus stretched out His hand and caught him, and said to him, "O you of little faith, why did you doubt?"

And when they got into the boat, the wind ceased. Matthew 14:31–32 NKJV

Come

Peter must have sensed a holy presence about Jesus the first time they met. Although Peter depended on earning his living by fishing, he dropped the nets from his strong, callused hands and accepted the mysterious, yet powerful, invitation from the Master:

"Follow me, and I will make you fishers of men."

Peter and his brother Andrew felt compelled by God to leave everything and follow Jesus. Nothing else mattered but to obey the call.

During his time with Jesus, Peter witnessed numerous miracles. It is no surprise that he loved and trusted Jesus more than anyone or anything. But he learned an unforgettable lesson of faith while being tossed about on the sea.

After Jesus fed the five thousand, He told the disciples to gather up the leftover food, leave immediately, and row to the other side of the water. Jesus would meet them there.

Peter and the others did as they were told. The sun was setting as they left shore. Peter knew from experience that the sea was not to be trusted. It could change at a moment's notice. Still, he followed his Master's instructions, and the disciples started rowing. Several miles out a storm arose. Waves higher than the fishing boat crashed around them.

Peter and the others struggled to keep the boat on course. No matter how hard they tried, they couldn't prevail against the violent winds and waves.

Peter had seen Jesus calm a storm once before when the Master was with them. Now the disciple felt abandoned and helpless. He had no idea Jesus had been praying on a mountainside and was watching the tossing fishing boat all along.

Time crept to just before dawn. Everyone struggled from exhaustion. Peter may well have been frantically bailing water or rowing with all his might when he glanced up and saw Someone walking on the water. Peter and the others were extremely afraid. They thought they saw a ghost and were preparing to die.

Over the roaring winds and waves, Peter heard a familiar voice. "Be of good cheer; it is I; be not afraid."

At that moment, Peter mustered all the love and courage he could find. "Lord, if it be thou, bid me come unto thee on the water," he cried.

So Jesus said, "Come."

Peter bravely climbed out of the boat and stepped out on the turbulent waves. His gaze remained firmly fixed on Jesus. Suddenly, he became distracted by the storm. He looked at the billowing waves. He felt whipped by the blasting winds. Panic took over and he started to sink.

"Lord, save me!" he shouted.

Peter instantly felt Someone grasp his hand and help him up.

Jesus said to Peter, "O thou of little faith, wherefore didst thou doubt?" After they climbed into the boat, the winds ceased and the sea grew calm.

We also hear God's call. When we follow, the sea of life may be as smooth as glass. But then the storms begin, and we are still determined to focus on Jesus.

When the storms worsen, we become frustrated and fear our lifeboat is out of control. In spite of all this, we must still remember to trust God's calling. We must keep our attention fixed on Him. As we do, Jesus guides us through the storms. He uses us to accomplish His purpose and brings us safely to the other shore. Even though we can't see Him or sense His presence, He is still there, helping and guiding.

The valuable lessons Peter learned from Jesus enabled him to mature into a great disciple. Peter's faith became the rock upon which God built His church.

In spite of our weaknesses, we can thank God for providing faith when He says "Come."

WHEN TO TALK, LISTEN, AND SERVE

The Lord God has given me his words of wisdom so that I may know what I should say to all these weary ones.

ISAIAH 50:4 TLB

COLD FEET, WARM HEART

Barbara glanced at the restaurant clock. Twelve-thirty in the morning. *Only half an hour to go,* she thought. She hurriedly completed her side work and thanked the Lord for a busy yet pleasant night and good tips. Now everything was strangely silent.

A man came in, sat down in her station, and ordered coffee. Barbara noticed how tired he looked. God often gave her an ability to understand the way people felt. This man, who was dressed in a navy blue uniform, appeared to have the weight of the world on his shoulders. Perhaps he did some sort of manual labor.

She completed her work and had a few extra moments to help the busboy clear and wipe down tables and chairs. Then she stole a glance at the man sipping his coffee. What words of cheer could she offer him?

It's really none of my business, she told herself. *Besides, I've always been careful. You never know nowadays.*

Barbara dismissed the thoughts and silently prayed for the man instead of saying anything.

One o'clock rolled around. She gave a final swish to a table and thanked her customer for coming in.

"Do you believe in God?" The man's voice trailed over her shoulder at almost a whisper.

Barbara stopped in her tracks and glanced toward the tired man.

"Do you believe in God?" he repeated, not looking up from the table.

She detected a tear slipping down his cheek. His shoulders started to tremble. He looked like he was trying not to break down.

Barbara felt her feet turn cold. She knew the Holy Spirit was coaxing her to tell the man about God's love, but she feared she would say the wrong thing.

She noticed he was not much older than her youngest son, probably only in his early twenties. The Lord had directed her to think about her son— and that was the only push she needed to overcome her initial fear. Barbara sat down across from the troubled young man, dishcloth still in her hand.

"Yes, I believe in God. He's my Savior and dearest friend. Why do you ask?"

She listened as the man proceeded to tell her through trembling lips how he and his young bride were expecting their first baby. Money for food and rent had become scarce since his wife could now only work part-time. Because she was very upset with him for not bringing in a better income, he had recently taken on a second job with a local trucking firm, loading, driving, and unloading the trucks. He explained how exhausted and discouraged he felt. Then he held out his worn hands with open cuts across his palms. He had no money to buy work gloves until he received his first paycheck.

"Do you know Jesus as your personal Savior?" she asked.

He nodded.

Barbara continued. "God can do anything to help us through our problems. He loves you and will meet your needs for money, strength, and encouragement. Just keep obeying and trusting Him."

Barbara paused. "Would you mind giving me your phone number? I know my husband would like to give you an extra pair of his work gloves."

A slight smile of gratitude crossed the man's face as he wrote his phone number on a slip of paper and handed it to Barbara.

The world seemed to stop in the restaurant as Barbara asked the man if he wanted her to pray with him. He nodded again. She felt the presence of the Holy Spirit as they prayed. Then Barbara stood and said good night.

Barbara and her husband were never able to get in touch with the man. The phone number he had given Barbara had been disconnected. Far from disappointed, though, they knew their work with him was finished. God would continue helping the man, even when they could not.

Barbara never forgot how God helped overcome her cold feet by using her warm heart. She was able to listen to someone's needs and tell how much God loved him. She never saw the young man again. It all seemed like a dream.

I wonder, she thought, *if this is how angels feel, or if this is what it is like to meet an angel unaware.*

I Love to Tell the Story

I love to tell the story—
More wonderful it seems
Than all the golden fancies
Of all the golden dreams;
I love to tell the story—
It did so much for me,
And that is just the reason
I tell it now to thee.

A. Katherine Hankey, 1834–1911

Apples of Gold

A word aptly spoken is like apples of gold in settings of silver.

Proverbs 25:11 NIV

Father, sometimes when You nudge me to tell someone about Your love, I focus on my apprehension instead of on Your leading. I feel my heart start to pound harder, my knees turn to jelly; and I get cold feet. I'm always afraid of saying or doing the wrong thing. Grant me wisdom during those times, I pray.

Thank You for how You help me overcome my fears and obey You. I'm grateful for You calling me to stop, listen, and help those around me. I praise You for granting me wisdom and graciousness, and for teaching me how to share the timely words of Your love and encouragement. Thank You for showing me when to talk, when to be silent and listen, and when to help.

Whenever I feel You nudge me to help another, I pray for You to provide treasured words of wisdom. Let them be as nourishing as golden apples in a silver basket. May all I say be uplifting and glorify You.

Called
to Pray

As followers of Jesus, we hear His call to help with many needs. At times, we may not give a second thought to heeding God's call. When we see a problem, it's natural to jump in and try to "fix" things. Instead, we need to seriously pray and seek God's will before we act. He may be calling us in a different direction.

Of all the ways God calls us, one of the most essential and valuable is when we are summoned to pray. Not a quick "Oh, by the way, Lord" prayer, but one where we labor in fervent supplication, with sincere submission before our heavenly Father.

Charles H. Spurgeon beautifully described genuine prayer that reaches the heart of God.

THE BELL-ROPE OF HEAVEN

Prayer pulls the rope below and the great bell rings above in the ears of God. Some scarcely stir the bell, for they pray so languidly; others give an occasional pluck at the rope; but he who wins with heaven is the man who grasps the rope boldly, and pulls continuously, with all his might.

HONORING GOD

I will bless the LORD at all times: his praise shall continually be in my mouth.

My soul shall make her boast in the
LORD: the humble shall hear thereof, and
be glad. PSALM 34:1–2 KJV

THE ONLY GIFT

What can we give God that He hasn't already given us? He provides us with life, our souls, and the bountiful blessings of living here on earth. There is only one thing we can give. With every ounce of our beings, we can give Him our praise—our whole-hearted, unconditional offering of thanksgiving.

We most often call on God when things go wrong. As the situation becomes urgent, we pray all the harder. Fear and discouragement tend to take over. How can we thank Him during such hopeless and troubled times?

When Paul and Silas were in prison (Acts 16), they had no idea whether they would see the light of day as they sat there, beaten and bound in chains. Still they prayed and sang hymns to the Lord.

Praise to God breaks our chains of fear and discouragement. Furthermore, praise to God helps us rise above our "hopeless" circumstances.

How can we praise Him when things seem so wrong? Try stuffing a piece of paper in your pocket and carry it with you everywhere you go. Focus on the goodness of God throughout the day, and on the many blessings, big and little, that He has bestowed on you in the past. Each time you think of a blessing, stop and write it down. It won't be long before that piece of paper is looking pretty dog-eared.

When you have a quiet time, pull out all your notes from several days and begin thanking God for His goodness. Then feel His wonderful, warm presence and the freedom He gives you!

Bless and praise Him at all times, no matter how hard things become. Thank Him for being your dearest friend, your source of strength. Exalt His name. Tell Him again and again He is Lord and Master in your life.

When you do this with a sincere heart, God will deliver you from your fears and direct you in the ways you are to go. Things may not always go your way, but you will see victory. He truly will help you through troubled times.

The more we lift Him up, the more God surrounds us with His unquenchable love. The more we lift Him up, the more He places His angels around us and delivers us and those we pray for from evil and harm.

Taste and see that God is good! Experience the blessings He has in store for you as you glorify and praise His name at *all* times.

PETITIONING GOD

Go, gather together all the Jews that are present in Shushan, and fast ye for me,

*and neither eat nor drink three days, night
or day: I also and my maidens will fast
likewise; and so will I go in unto the king,
which is not according to the law: and if I
perish, I perish.* ESTHER 4:16 KJV

ANYTIME, ANYWHERE

Hadassah had no idea how brave God would require her to be in the very near future. For starters, though, God was calling her to leave the security of her home. Since both of her parents had died, she had been living with her cousin, Mordecai, who was like a father to her. Now she had to leave him. Hadassah was being summoned to the harem of King Ahasuerus of Persia.

Hadassah must have trembled as she entered the king's luxurious palace. She would never forget the lessons Mordecai had taught her about being faithful to the one true God. She carefully followed her cousin's advice to hide her identity as a Jew so she would be safe.

When Hadassah entered the royal harem, her name was immediately changed to Esther, a name that meant star of Venus. Such a name was chosen because Esther was a very beautiful woman.

Certainly Esther's loveliness and grace had won King Ahasuerus's heart. And Esther knew he loved her above all others. It wasn't long before she was crowned queen.

Soon Queen Esther discovered how much a courtier named Haman hated her cousin Mordecai. Haman was angry because Mordecai had refused to bow down to him. The enraged Haman decided to get even. After cunningly convincing the king to give him his signet ring, Haman decreed all Jews were to be killed.

When Mordecai sent this dire news to Esther, she knew she had to be true to her people and her God. She sent a message to Mordecai for all their people to fast and pray.

"Go, gather together all the Jews that are present in Shushan, and fast ye for me, and neither eat nor drink three days, night or day: I also and my maidens will fast likewise; and so will I go in unto the king, which is not according to the law: and if I perish, I perish."

In spite of her fear, Esther decided to reveal her Jewish identity to her husband. After three days of fasting and praying, she approached the king. She knew she was risking her life in doing so. If he would not receive her, Esther could be put to death. But God showed favor to Esther. The king held out his golden scepter, and Esther touched the top of it.

Esther launched into her plan by inviting her husband and Haman to a banquet. After the first sumptuous meal, she insisted on a second banquet.

Shortly after Esther's second invitation, the king was reviewing some historical records. When he read how Mordecai had once saved his life, he immediately ordered Haman to honor Mordecai. Haman reluctantly did as the king requested.

Time for the second banquet arrived. During the meal, King Ahasuerus asked Esther what she petitioned of him. Esther told her husband about Haman's evil command. She begged him for her safety as a Jew, and for protection of her people. Haman was caught in his own lies. The king ordered Haman hanged on the gallows intended for Mordecai.

King Ahasuerus then gave his signet ring to Mordecai, and Esther appointed her cousin to be in charge of the house of Haman.

Esther once more pleaded before the king as she fell, weeping at his feet. She implored him to counteract Haman's order to kill the Jews.

"If it please the king, and if I have found favour in his sight, and the thing seem right before the king, and I be pleasing in his eyes, let it be written to reverse the letters devised by Haman the son of Hammedatha the Agagite, which he wrote to destroy the Jews which are in all the king's provinces.

"For how can I endure to see the evil that shall come unto my people? or how can I endure to see the destruction of my kindred?"

Unfortunately, Haman's deadly order could not be reversed by law. But the king did give permission to Esther and Mordecai to do what they could.

Esther surely must have returned to her Lord in prayer, while Mordecai decreed that the Jews would be allowed to fight for their lives. With

God's help, the Jews won an overwhelming victory and were saved.

Esther's passionate prayers, faithful acknowledgment of God's directions, and her unswerving willingness to serve Him anytime, anywhere, were rewarded. In spite of the loss of her parents and her separation from the security and love of her cousin Mordecai's home, the Lord blessed Esther with the love of a king and the salvation of her people. He also made it possible for her to be with Mordecai again.

FASTING AND PRAYER

"But you, when you fast, anoint your head and wash your face so that your fasting will not be noticed by men, but by your Father who is in secret; and your Father who sees what is done in secret will reward you." MATTHEW 6:17–18 NAS

DECREASE TO INCREASE

When we struggle with difficulties, we are often required to dig deeper in our prayer lives. One way of doing this is by fasting.

Some describe fasting as not only increasing our communion with God, but also decreasing our waistlines. This is probably true, but I look at it more regarding our relationship with God.

While fasting by itself takes off some excess poundage, it is ineffective spiritually unless joined with sincere, ardent prayer. Sometimes when we fast, we may feel like our poor bodies are dying from hunger. Likewise, our souls must abstain from our own desires and notions and be open to what God is trying to teach us. When we unconditionally give our all to God, we allow Him to bathe us inside and out with His pure, cleansing water.

The most awesome part is how God ministers to us during this time of prayer and fasting. He calls us to take our urgent cares to Him and plead our cause. Sometimes we beg on behalf of others. Often we pray for them to give their lives to the Lord. Each of us, however, has a free will.

As we pray for others, we must acknowledge that each of us has his or her own individual relationship with God. Each person has to be accountable to God. Though difficult, we must be willing to let go of those we pray for and allow God to work directly in their lives. He is able to accomplish far more than we are capable of doing.

Oh, how we labor in prayer for our dear ones to accept and experience such abundant life in Him! And how grand it is when our prayers are answered!

We may see immediate results to our prayers, or we may continue waiting, praying, and fasting. Sometimes the answers seem never to come. During those times, *know for sure who is in charge*. God is in control. He is all-knowing and all-powerful. He doesn't work according to our time clock or our will. No matter how things may look, His wisdom surpasses all understanding.

He loves and cares for us. He loves and cares for those we bring before Him in prayer. We are His children. He really does listen to our prayers. In His infinite timing and wisdom, He sets His plan into motion and takes all things, working them together for good.

During our prayer and fasting, our minds often turn from our burdens to the wonderful presence of God. As our will decreases and God's will increases, His presence fills our souls to overflowing. Then He can unfold His spiritual mysteries and wisdom before us.

When we pray and fast and wait on Him, He renews our strength. He changes and empowers our lives so that we can go forward. He helps us stop burying ourselves under the circumstances. We learn to overcome the same circumstances through Christ Jesus and see victories won.

FOLLOWING GOD'S ORDERS

"That all the peoples of the earth may know the hand of the LORD, that it is mighty, that you may fear the LORD your God forever." JOSHUA 4:24 NKJV

STEPS OF OBEDIENCE

Because he was obedient to all the Lord asked of him, Joshua was God's choice to lead the people across the Jordan River and around the walls of Jericho. Even Joshua's name depicted God's call in his life. Joshua means "servant of the Lord" or "one with a special calling." Indeed, a great deal of communication went on between Joshua and God before Joshua led the children of Israel to victory.

Joshua's hope for courage and triumph was solely dependent upon his unwavering trust and obedience to God. So before Joshua and his people moved forward, they were instructed by God to do one essential thing. They were to sanctify themselves outwardly and allow God to cleanse them inwardly. Not the smallest thing could come between them and God in order for Him to work.

Joshua and the children of Israel did as their Lord instructed. Now they were ready to move forward. Before they did, though, God cautioned Joshua to have the people walk a distance behind the ark of the covenant carried by the priests. The ark represented the presence of God. They must not go ahead of His leading.

Joshua and the children of Israel moved toward the Jordan River. The priests carrying the ark of the covenant led the way. At that time, the Jordan River was at flood stage and overflowing its banks. How would they ever be able to cross the treacherous waters?

Trust in God overcame fear as the people watched the priests step into the raging currents. The moment the priests' feet touched the water, the river rose in a huge heap about thirty miles upstream from where the Israelites were about to cross.

The priests faithfully marched forward, bearing the ark on their shoulders. They stopped at a certain spot and stood firm on the now-dry riverbed while all of Israel hurried past them. The priests would remain on the riverbed until everyone safely arrived on the other shore. (Some scholars speculate that between all the tribes—men, women, children, and servants—approximately two million people, along with their livestock, crossed the Jordan that day.)

After the children of Israel had safely reached the other side, Joshua followed the Lord's next command. He selected one man from each of the twelve tribes to return to the still-dry river. Each man hastily obeyed instructions to carry a rock on his shoulder from the Jordan to its shore, where the people waited. The men lugged the heavy stones out and set them down.

Joshua walked to where the priests stood on the riverbed and began gathering twelve other large stones. The Israelites watched as their leader built a monument of thanksgiving to God.

Afterward, the priests carried the ark out of the river and stepped onto the shore. The Israelites were amazed as they witnessed the mighty Jordan reclaim its territory. Huge waves rolled over the area they had just safely walked over and flooded its banks.

Joshua took the other twelve stones the men had carried to shore and built a second monument to God. After he finished, he told the people:

> *"When your children shall ask their fathers in time to come, saying, What mean these stones? Then ye shall let your children know, saying, Israel came over this Jordan on dry land.*
>
> *"For the LORD your God dried up the waters of Jordan from before you, until ye were passed over, as the LORD your God did to the Red sea, which he dried up from before us, until we were gone over:*
>
> *"That all the people of the earth might know the hand of the LORD, that it is mighty: that ye might fear the LORD your God for ever."*

MOVING FORWARD WITH GOD

The seventh time around [the city], when the priests sounded the trumpet blast, Joshua commanded the people, "Shout! For the LORD has given you the city! The

city and all that is in it are to be devoted
to the LORD." JOSHUA 6:16–17 NIV

SHOUTS OF TRIUMPH

The Israelites set up camp at Gilgal, on Jordan's shore. Their tents rested on Jericho's forbidding border. Once they were settled, Joshua passed on God's next instructions to purify themselves outwardly and allow God to cleanse each of them within.

One day, Joshua was standing near Jericho when a man appeared before him. From where did this stranger come? The man stood opposite Joshua, His sword drawn.

Joshua went up to the man and was ready to defend himself. "Art thou for us, or for our adversaries?"

"Nay," replied the man, "but as Captain of the host of the LORD am I now come."

Joshua knew at that moment the man was sent by God and he fell to the ground. Barely daring to look up, he asked what God would have him do.

The Captain of the Lord's host spoke to Joshua with full authority. "Loose thy shoe from off thy foot; for the place whereon thou standest is holy."

The Lord promised Joshua that Jericho was in His hands. He went on to give him important instructions on how to move forward: "Ye shall compass the city, all ye men of war, and go round about the city once. Thus shalt thou do six days.

"And it shall come to pass, that when they make a long blast with the ram's horn, and when ye hear the sound of the trumpet, all the people shall shout with a great shout; and the wall of the city shall fall down flat, and the people shall ascend up every man straight before him."

Joshua gave the instructions to begin the march with trumpets blowing all the way. Day one, day two, and on through day six they marched, one time around the city each day.

Some historians believe Jericho covered about eight and a half acres. There were two walls surrounding the city, one next to the other. The thickness of the inner wall is said to have been approximately twelve feet, the thickness of the outside one about six feet, and the height may have been about seventy yards.

Many geologists believe the power causing the walls to tumble could have been as great as the San Francisco earthquake of 1906 and as strong as blasts of dynamite. Did the vibration from the marching and blowing of rams' horns work the rocks in the huge walls and cause them to fall? We don't have all the answers, but one thing is certain. God moved His mighty hand, and the walls fell flat!

Joshua and the Lord's people experienced victory beyond description or comprehension. Why? Because they were faithful to God.

Marching on Our Knees

Make a joyful shout to God, all the earth!
Sing out the honor of His name;
Make His praise glorious.

Say to God,
"How awesome are Your works!
Through the greatness of Your power
Your enemies shall submit themselves to You.

"All the earth shall worship You
And sing praises to You;
They shall sing praises to Your name."
Selah   PSALM 66:1–4 NKJV

One Step at a Time

Sometimes God doesn't ask us to do anything but draw apart and pray. Our prayer concerns may not be about big or urgent matters, or they may regard circumstances that are absolutely overwhelming, even hopeless. Either way, every single prayer is important to God, as are we.

Christians have been known to storm the gates of heaven, demanding (or commanding) that their needs be granted. I speak from personal experience. There are times when I have begged and pleaded for my petitions to be answered in a certain way. I felt I knew what was best. God showed me otherwise.

When children demand their way, they usually don't get very far with their parents. Instead, they are taught to talk, listen, trust, and obey. They gradually learn who is really in charge and what is best.

I believe the simple keys to effective prayer are two-way communication with God and total obedience and submission to His will—not ours. We must remember God sees the whole picture. He is all-wise and all-knowing. He understands us and those we care about beyond our comprehension! Not only does He know us, but He loves us with an endless, unconditional love.

Think of the seven trips the Israelites made around Jericho. What an outrageous thing to do! Marching and praising God by blowing rams' horns with no weapons drawn. Waiting and obeying.

Consider seven ways to approach God's glorious throne of grace. We come humbly on bended knees before the almighty creator, the One who made us. We enter His presence as though we are standing on holy ground. Our Lord of lords, king of all kings, the mighty ruler of all. Who are we that God should be mindful of us, except for His mercy and grace?

1. Praise and adore Him. Give God the one thing He hasn't already given you: your worship and thanksgiving. We take so many of His bountiful blessings for granted. It pleases Him when we pause to thank Him for what He has already done for us.

Tell Him about your joys, even the funny things in your life. Surely God has a sense of humor. (He made some pretty funny-looking animals, right?)

When we are discouraged and suffer from despair, we often find it difficult to think of praises. Try remembering the sunrise that morning, a bird chirping outside your window, or even the cleansing rain of last night. See how one little prayer of thanksgiving cracks open the door to heaven and God's love is revealed.

2. Acknowledge His presence. There are times we may not feel Him near any more than we are able to see Him. Still, we must take that tiny step of faith and thank God for being with us.

3. Repent of wrongdoing and allow Him to cleanse your heart. Often, when we bring our burdens to the Lord, they are accompanied by hurt, anger, bitterness, and many other things that can hinder God's work. While we may think we have a right to these feelings, we need to release them to God. When we do, He cleanses and soothes our souls and begins the process of healing our aching hearts.

4. Present your needs to Him. Tell Him about your disappointments and concerns, big and small. Explain your problems and worries.

5. Wait on His answers and solutions. Sometimes while we linger, we may feel like the Israelites wandering in the wilderness. We wonder what we can do. All may seem hopeless.

   We may have to wait a few hours or days for answered prayer. Other times, it takes weeks, months, or even years. What if we don't see some prayers answered in our earthly lifetime? No matter how long we wait, we can be assured our prayers are being lifted to God now and for eternity.

   At times we feel like we're losing. We want to take our spiritual marbles and go home. Don't lose heart. God is still on the throne. We must trust Him for His timing and wisdom. He knows what is best. He alone is in charge.

6. Thank Him ahead of time for His answers to come. *When the world crashes down around us and evil presses in on all sides, we can steady our shaky knees, raise our voices in praise, and thank Him for taking control of every situation we*

trust to Him. (Paraphrased from Hebrews 12:12 TLB.)

Romans 8:28 assures us we can know all that happens to us is for our good, if we love God, are fitting into His plans, and following His lead.

7. When God gives the go-ahead, march forward. Praise Him every step of the way with all your being. Even though life's problems loom before us like the towering walls of Jericho, and we want to shrink from fear and discouragement, we must remember we are not fighting these battles. God is. We are not alone. Our job is to trust in Him, lean completely on Him, and draw from His strength.

   Keep marching and praying on your knees. The spiritual rocks shifting in your walls of Jericho from your prayer steps with God may not be visible for some time. But be assured that a pure, unselfish prayer of a righteous individual avails much!

   As we pray, praise, trust, and obey, we can be confident God is the victor. He alone is the author and finisher of all!

BATTLE HYMN OF THE REPUBLIC

He has sounded forth the trumpet
    that shall never call retreat;
He is sifting out the hearts of men
    before His judgment-seat.
Oh, be swift, my soul, to answer Him!
    be jubilant, my feet!
Our God is marching on.

Glory, glory, hallelujah!
Glory, glory, hallelujah!
Glory, glory, hallelujah!
His truth is marching on.

JULIA WARD HOWE, 1819–1910

YOU ARE MY ROCK!

Heavenly Father, as I bring my cares to You, I fully trust You to handle them in Your own way. I love You, Lord. You are my rock and my strength. You are my fortress and my rescuer. In You I will put all my trust.

Each day I call upon You, who are worthy of my praise. Each day I need not fear, for I know You battle on my behalf against the forces of such an evil world.

When pangs of illness and death surround me, and when torrents of ungodliness assail me, I flee to Your open arms. There, You are ready to hear and help me.

I will trust in You, Lord, rather than my own understanding. In every circumstance I will acknowledge You. For You, Lord, direct my paths. The joy You give me from Your love is my strength. I thank You and praise You for Your loving-kindness!

In Jesus' name, amen.

GOD'S CLEAR CALL

And He said to them, "Go into all the world and preach the gospel to every creature." MARK 16:15 NKJV

Shortly after I heard God calling me to write, I went to a women's retreat. While there, I felt Him speak to my heart about the heavy responsibility a Christian writer carries.

The realization that my words would influence others was overwhelming. Even though I had already dedicated my writing to the Lord, I felt a deep need to ask Him for insight and wisdom.

Then, one Sunday night, among church friends meeting in a home for prayer and Bible study, I shared my need. I asked our group to pray for me.

Quietly and reverently, they gathered around and I was anointed with oil. Together, we brought my request to the Lord. I felt humbled before God, ready and willing to be His servant in any way He wanted.

After we prayed, there wasn't a bolt of lightning or an emotional thrill. Just a calm, warm assurance of His presence.

I knew He would guide my hand.

Now I pray:

The LORD bless you and keep you;
The LORD make His face shine upon you,
And be gracious to you;
The LORD lift up His countenance upon you,
And give you peace. NUMBERS 6:24–26 NKJV

The LORD shall preserve your going out
and your coming in From this time forth,
and even forevermore. PSALM 121:8 NKJV

OTHER BOOKS BY
ANITA CORRINE DONIHUE

If you enjoyed *When I Hear His Call,* be sure to look for these ot[...]
books by Anita Corrine Donihue at your local Christian booksto[...]

When I'm on My Knees
Anita's first book, focusing on prayer, has sold nearly
a half-million copies.
ISBN 1-55748-976-9 . . . . $4.97

When I'm Praising God . . . .
Anita's sequel to *When I'm on My Knees,* promoting
praise as the key to a fulfilling Christian life.
ISBN 1-57748-447-9 . . . . $4.97

When I'm in His Presence
Anita's third book, encouraging women to look for
God's working in their everyday lives.
ISBN 1-57748-665-X $4.97

When God Sees Me Through
Anita's fourth book in the series, celebrating the Lord's
faithfulness through every circumstance of our lives.
ISBN 1-57748-977-2 . . . . $4.97

ALSO AVAILABLE:
When I'm on My Knees Prayer Journal
Favorite selections from *When I'm on My Knees,*
plus ample journaling space for your prayer requests
and praise notes.
ISBN 1-57748-836-9 . . . . $4.97

Available wherever books are sold.
Or order from:

Barbour Publishing, Inc.
P.O. Box 719
Uhrichsville, OH 44683
www.barbourbooks.com

If you order by mail, add $2.00 to your order for shipping.
Prices are subject to change without notice.